John Tyler

10th President of the United States

A proud Virginian, John Tyler served as his state's governor as well as a U.S. representative and senator before becoming the 10th President of the United States. (Library of Congress.)

John Tyler

10th President of the United States

Lucille Falkof

 GARRETT EDUCATIONAL CORPORATION

Cover: *Official presidential photographic portrait of John Tyler by George P. A. Healy.* (Copyrighted by the White House Historical Association; photograph by the National Geographic Society.)

Manufactured in the United States of America

Edited and produced by Synthegraphics Corporation

Library of Congress Cataloging in Publication Data

Falkof, Lucille, 1924-
   John Tyler, 10th president of the United States / Lucille Falkof.
      p.   cm. — (Presidents of the United States)
   Includes bibliographical references.
   Summary: Presents the life of John Tyler, including his childhood, education, employment, and political career.
   1. Tyler, John, 1790–1862—Juvenile literature.
2. Presidents—United States—Biography—Juvenile literature.   3. United States—Politics and government—1841–1845—Juvenile literature.   [1. Tyler, John, 1790–1862. 2. Presidents.]   I. Title   II. Title: John Tyler, tenth president of the United States. III. Series.
E397.F35   1990
973.5'8'092—dc20
[B]
[92]   89-39951
ISBN 0-944483-60-7   CIP
                                                                AC

Contents

Chronology for John Tyler

1790 Born on March 29

1807 Graduated from the College of William and Mary

1809 Admitted to Virginia bar

1811–1816 Served five terms in the Virginia House of Delegates

1813 Married Letitia Christian on March 29

1817–1821 Served in United States House of Representatives

1825–1827 Served as governor of Virginia

1827 Elected to United States Senate

1836 Resigned from Senate; defeated in bid for vice-presidency

1840 Elected Vice-President on Harrison-Tyler ticket

1841 Assumed presidency on April 6 upon death of President William Henry Harrison

1842 Letitia Tyler died on September 10

1844 Married Julia Gardiner on June 26

1845 On March 1 signed joint resolution of Congress for annexation of Texas

1861 Elected president of a peace convention in February; urged secession of Virginia at a state convention in March and April; elected to House of Representatives of the Confederacy in November

1862 Died on January 18

Chapter 1

A Secret Mission

It was dark and quite late, after 10:30 P.M., when the Washington train to New York pulled into the station. Four men emerged from the train. One was John Lorimer Graham, postmaster of the city of New York; the second was Robert Rantoul, a Boston politician. The third was a tall, slender, middle-aged man, John Tyler, President of the United States. He was escorted by his son, John Tyler, Jr.

By the time the four men arrived at their hotel, the owner had already dismissed his servants for the night. He had promised the men that the purpose of their trip to New York would not leak out, and he was determined to keep his word.

A QUIET ELOPEMENT

On the following day, June 26, 1844, the weather was hot and sultry, but nothing seemed to dampen the high spirits of the President, for he was about to secretly elope with a beautiful young woman. In a quiet and intimate ceremony at the Church of the Ascension at 2:00 P.M., the 54-year-old President married Julia Gardiner, age 24. The only other guests besides the three men with Tyler were the immediate members of the bride's family.

There was no doubt that the President was going to be much envied when the secret marriage was revealed, for Julia Gardiner was not only young and beautiful but intelligent as well. She had been a reigning belle in Washington society and belonged to a prominent and wealthy New York family. The bride was dressed simply and elegantly, but she wore no jewelry, for her family was still in mourning following the tragic death of her father four months earlier.

The News Leaks Out

After the ceremony, the guests drove in five carriages to the Gardiner residence on Lafayette Place for a light meal. By the time the newlyweds arrived at the ferry slip to cross the Hudson River to the New Jersey side for the train to Philadelphia, the news of their marriage had already leaked out. A noisy group of local politicians and Tyler supporters awaited them on the ferryboat to greet and congratulate them.

It did not take long for word of the happy event to make newspaper headlines all over the country. One newspaperman called the President "Lucky Honest John," but others were not as charitable. There were those who were shocked that the President had taken a new wife so soon after the death of his first wife. And there were well-intentioned friends who, during the courtship, had questioned Tyler's marrying a woman whose *mother* was nine years younger than himself.

One friend, Henry A. Wise, cautioned Tyler, "You are not only past middle age, but you are President of the United States, and that is a dazzling dignity which may charm a damsel more than the man she marries."

Tyler had laughed and insisted, "Why, my dear sir, I am just full in my prime."

An Affectionate Wife

Three years later, Mr. Wise was to agree with Tyler when he noticed among Tyler's family baggage a double-seated wicker baby carriage. Seven children were produced by the Tyler-Gardiner marriage, much to Tyler's delight.

Despite the difference in their ages, the marriage turned

out to be a loving and happy one, and Julia lavished great affection on her husband. At one point, her mother was forced to advise her not to caress the President so much lest he might neglect his presidential duties. Even Julia's sister, Margaret, scolded her for kissing her husband in front of other people. Julia and the children brought the greatest happiness to Tyler's later years.

A REVOLUTIONARY HERITAGE

John Tyler's birth on March 29, 1790, marked the arrival of the fifth generation of Tylers in America. The first was Henry Tyler, who left England about the time King Charles I was defeated and the Puritans gained control of the country. In January 1653, Henry obtained a grant for 254 acres of land on what would later become the city of Williamsburg, the first capital of Virginia. By the time the future President Tyler was born, the family's fortune had grown considerably.

John Tyler was named after his father, a man already prominent in the new nation's affairs by the time of his son's birth. The elder Tyler and his friend, Thomas Jefferson, were law students in the spring of 1765 when they drifted into Williamsburg to hear a young firebrand, Patrick Henry, deliver a passionate speech against King George III and the Stamp Act (a tax imposed on the American colonies in 1765 by the English Parliament). The speech so impressed Tyler that he became an ardent champion for the cause of independence.

Judge Tyler

The father, like his son later on, was educated at the College of William and Mary and began his career as a lawyer. He was called Judge Tyler after he was appointed to a state court. The judge was a zealous patriot, and on several occasions during the Revolutionary War, he risked his life and his property for the cause of independence.

After Judge Tyler was elected a member of the Virginia House of Delegates (the state legislature), he played an important part in starting the movement that led to the Constitutional Convention in Philadelphia in 1787. He believed in strengthening the original Articles of Confederation (the first American constitution, adopted in 1781) in order to regulate trade among the states, but he was horrified when the convention created instead a new federal political system. He even tried to block ratification of the new Constitution on the grounds that it gave too much power to the central government and did not adequately protect the rights of the individual states. Many years later, Judge Tyler's son would fight for these very same principles.

A Loving Childhood

The future President was born into a family that was well educated and affluent. Their home was a 1,200-acre plantation called "Greenway." Besides the main house of six large rooms, there were such buildings as a kitchen, laundry, meathouse, ice house, two carriage houses, 20 stalls for horses, and accommodations for 40 slaves. It was here, at Greenway, in Charles City County, Virginia, that John Tyler, the sixth of eight children, was born and raised.

Young John's childhood was similar to that of other sons of the Virginia aristocracy. He was surrounded by wealth and lavished with affection. His mother's death when he was seven years old was a severe emotional blow to the young boy, and Judge Tyler showered his son with love to make up for the loss. The judge was an affectionate and sympathetic parent whom President Tyler remembered fondly. He would describe how the judge would sit on the lawn at Greenway, telling tall stories about the great American Revolution or playing his violin for the plantation children. Young John also loved music and learned "to fiddle." It was a relaxing hobby that he enjoyed, especially in his post-presidential years.

On the surface, John seemed to be a gentle and amiable youngster. He had the ability to handle people and difficult situations with kindness and tact, a part of his personality that would remain with him all of his life.

A Student Revolt

But outward appearances can be deceiving. Many people who came in contact with young John failed to recognize the firmness of character and the fire that could blaze when the occasion merited it. One of the few stories told about Tyler's youth relates to his experiences with a local schoolteacher, a Mr. McMurdo, who was a tyrant. As Tyler recalled later, "it was a wonder that he did not whip all the sense out of his scholars."

One day, when the young lads could stand it no longer, the students revolted. The leader of the rebellion was 10-year-old John Tyler. The students threw McMurdo down, tied his hands and feet, and locked the schoolroom door. It was late afternoon before a passerby heard his cries and released him.

The indignant teacher reported the incident to Judge Tyler and demanded that the young rebel be given his due punishment. But the judge, who himself hated any form of tyranny, replied, *"Sic semper tyrannis"* (Latin for "Thus it is always with tyrants"). Then he sent the schoolteacher on his way. The judge was probably secretly delighted to see such spirit in his normally gentle son.

A SERIOUS SCHOLAR

At age 12, young John entered the preparatory program at the College of William and Mary. A year or so later, he began the regular college curriculum. Most of his subjects dealt with English literature and the study of the Greek and Latin languages. But he was also introduced to history and economics. In his economics class, a new text was used. It was written by an Englishman, Adam Smith, and was called *Wealth of Nations*. This work made a great impact on the young student.

Adam Smith argued that individual enterprise should be encouraged and that the government should not interfere with trade. Smith's ideas meshed later with the South's views, and with those of Tyler and his father. Both men believed that each state had the right to make its own decisions on such questions as trade and tariffs (taxes on imported goods).

In 1807, a few months after his 17th birthday, John Tyler graduated from college. At his commencement he made an eloquent address on "Female Education," a rather radical subject for its day. It won the unanimous approval of the college faculty, who deemed it "the best commencement oration, both in style and matter, ever delivered at that institution within their recollection."

John was a very serious and oftentimes moody young man. He had a slight build, silky brown hair, and a long, thin, aristocratic-looking face, with high cheekbones and a rather large Roman nose. He was always much too thin and suffered frequent colds and severe stomach problems all his life.

Studying Law

With his undergraduate years behind him, John proceeded to follow in his father's footsteps. He began the study of law, first with his father, then with his cousin, Samuel Taylor. When his father became governor of Virginia in 1809, the family moved to the new capital at Richmond. John then studied with Edmund Randolph, who had been attorney general of the United States in Washington's administration.

Randolph had a reputation as a brilliant lawyer, but the young Mr. Tyler was dismayed by Randolph's views on Federalism, a political philosophy that called for a strong central government. Tyler was shocked by Randolph's arguments in favor of "a supreme executive, a supreme legislature and a supreme judiciary and a power in Congress to veto laws." All of these ideas were in complete opposition to all of his father's ideas on states' rights and those of his professors at William and Mary.

A Distinguished Visitor

John was now living in the governor's mansion with his family, but he was hardly living in elegant surroundings. Though called "the palace," the governor's home was merely a two-story wooden building, badly in need of repair. Despite its shabby and cramped accommodations, the Tyler family enjoyed some great moments there. One was a visit by Thomas Jefferson.

In October 1809, shortly after his retirement from the presidency, Jefferson accepted an invitation for dinner from his old friend, Governor Tyler. Young John took charge of the arrangements, determined that every courtesy be extended to their distinguished guest. He even ordered *two* plum puddings for the occasion. The governor was very surprised when the desserts were set upon the table. He questioned whether this was not just a bit extraordinary, to which his son replied, "Yes, but *this* is an extraordinary occasion."

YOUNG MAN IN A HURRY

By the time he had turned 21, John Tyler was already practicing law. He had been admitted to the Virginia bar in 1809. In that same year, 1811, he was elected to the Virginia House of Delegates. As a lawyer, he quickly gained a reputation as a brilliant courtroom performer. In those days, criminal law made up the bulk of a lawyer's practice. In the beginning, Tyler took many near-hopeless cases in order to gain practice in the fine art of oration before a judge and jury. He quickly learned that the way to a juror's heart was more often based on feelings and emotions than on law and reason. In time, he became known as one of the great orators of his day.

John earned his reputation in the House of Delegates almost immediately. There were two key issues on which he spoke. One dealt with the renewal of the charter for the Bank of the United States. The second centered on whether a U.S. senator, at that time elected by each state's legislature rather than by the people at large, had the right to vote against the set instructions of his legislature.

The National Bank Issue

In 1791, when the new nation was starting out under the federal Constitution, Alexander Hamilton, Washington's secretary of the treasury, decided that the country needed to create a national bank. The bank would issue standard monies in place of the many state currencies then being used. The bank would also serve as a depository for the funds collected from taxes and tariffs and thereby back the national currency. The charter would also allow the bank to establish branch banks in the main commercial cities of several states. (Since the South was mostly agricultural, most of these commercial cities were in the North.) At that time, the issue was hotly debated.

Thomas Jefferson, another member of Washington's Cabinet, argued that nothing in the Constitution gave the government the right to establish such a bank. Hamilton pointed out that the constitutional power granted to Congress to collect taxes and regulate trade "implied" that it was constitutional to create a bank in which to deposit the money collected through taxes and tariffs. Hamilton's interpretation was a "loose construction" of the words in the Constitution. Jefferson insisted, on the other hand, that if the words were not specifically written in the Constitution, no such power was granted. This was called a "strict construction" of the Constitution. These two points of view would be argued for years to come. Washington accepted Hamilton's argument, and the first national bank was chartered in 1791 for a period of 20 years.

Senators Disobey

For Judge Tyler, the creation of the Bank of the United States supported his worst fears that a strong federal government would take over responsibilities that he believed were better left to the states. Now, in 1811, the bank's charter was up for renewal. The Virginia legislature had "instructed" its U.S. senators to vote against the renewal. However, both men, William Giles and Richard Brent, disobeyed their orders and voted for the renewal. Even though the Senate had killed the bank renewal bill in February, young John Tyler was determined to right what he considered to be two wrongs.

Tyler was convinced that the Bank of the United States was unconstitutional, and he believed strongly that the Virginia senators had defied the legislature and therefore the authority of the "sovereign" or independent state of Virginia. He offered resolutions censuring Brent for voting for the recharter and Giles for not following the instructions of the legislature. The resolutions were sent to committee, amended a bit, and then passed by the House of Delegates, 97–20, a heady victory for the new member of the legislature.

Tyler's law practice was now paying him $2,000 a year, a large sum for those days. And because his political career was also firmly established, he could now begin to think about taking a wife.

Chapter 2

Lawyer, Legislator, and Family Man

John Tyler had met the lovely Letitia Christian at a neighborhood party shortly after his graduation from the College of William and Mary. Letitia's home, "Cedar Grove," was on the road between Greenway and Richmond. When Governor Tyler resigned in 1811 and returned to Greenway, his son, John, traveled from Richmond to Greenway on a fairly regular basis. During the journey, he often stopped at the Christian home, and in time, the friendship of John and Letitia flowered into love.

A BIRTHDAY WEDDING

Letitia was a shy, quiet girl, and their courtship tended to be a sedate and proper affair. Indeed, the young lover admitted he had not even dared to kiss the hand of his bride-to-be until three weeks before the wedding. After their marriage on March 29 (John's birthday), 1813, John brought his bride to a beautiful 500-acre section of Greenway that had been given to him by his father.

Letitia had no real interest in politics, preferring instead the domestic life of taking care of her children, supervising the household slaves with kindness, and tending her exquisite gardens. As Tyler moved up on the political ladder, Letitia preferred to stay at home. Although their marriage was a happy one for 29 years, it gave off none of the sparks and excitement of Tyler's later marriage to Julia Gardiner.

A BRIEF MILITARY FLING

During the War of 1812, John Tyler had a brief opportunity to vent his hate of the British, which had been instilled in him by his father. In the summer of 1813, when the British captured and plundered the town of Hampton, the patriotic fervor of the people of Virginia was aroused. When Tyler heard rumors that the British were about to march up the James River and attack the state capital at Richmond, he joined a military unit and was commissioned a captain.

Though he knew absolutely nothing about military science, Captain Tyler took a group of local farmers and, by using a simple drill, shaped them into a fairly disciplined unit. The unit was ordered to Williamsburg and quartered at the College of William and Mary.

A False Alarm

One night, while the men in the unit were sound asleep, a cry erupted, "The British are in town!" Panic-stricken, the men struggled in the darkness to get down the stairs and escape. In their mad rush, they fell down the steps and landed in a heap at the bottom. The rumor turned out to be false. The British left the area shortly after, and the farmers of Tyler's unit happily returned home.

Tyler's military career lasted exactly two months. The brief military fling earned him the title of "Captain" and a veteran's right to claim some western lands. When he was President, some of his Whig enemies ridiculed his brief military record by calling him "Captain Tyler" instead of President. Many years later, after the Civil War, conditions for the Tyler family would be so poor that his widow, Julia, would deem herself fortunate to have the monthly bonus of eight dollars awarded by Congress to widows of the veterans of the War of 1812.

ON TO WASHINGTON

In 1816, at the close of the War of 1812, Tyler was elected on a states' rights platform to the United States House of Representatives from the Richmond district. Living conditions in the mudhole called Washington were wretched. The nation's capital consisted of muddy lanes where hogs and cows shared the streets with people. The swamp areas bred malaria and other fevers. Even on the one main thoroughfare, Pennsylvania Avenue, people could not walk at night because there were not enough funds for fuel to light street lamps.

While Congress was in session, Tyler lived in Washington, but his wife and children remained at home in far more comfortable and familiar surroundings. With an ever-growing family to maintain, Tyler could only afford to live in a boardinghouse, as did most of his fellow congressmen. Letitia visited the city only once before the family moved to Washington after her husband became President.

Tyler moved swiftly into Washington society. As the son of a state governor and a member of a prominent Virginia family, he was invited often to the makeshift home of President James Madison and his charming wife, Dolley.

The White House was not being used at that time because it had been burned by the British during the War of 1812 and was in the process of being rebuilt. However, this did not deter Mrs. Madison from entertaining her guests at elegant dinners. Unfortunately for Tyler's sensitive stomach, Dolley's love of highly seasoned French food nearly ruined his digestive system, though he did admit that he loved Dolley's generous use of fine champagne.

Maiden Speech

Tyler's first speech in the House was important because it firmly set a principle of behavior which he not only believed in but acted upon throughout his long political career. He was determined that he would never sacrifice his beliefs in order to be popular. In his maiden speech in the House of Representatives, he said, "Popularity, I have always thought, may aptly be compared to a coquette—the more you woo her, the more apt she is to elude your embrace." He refused to listen to "mere buzz or clamor," only to the "voice of a majority of the people."

But Tyler warned that he would not listen to his constituents if they demanded that he violate the Constitution. "My constituents have no right to violate the Constitution themselves," he said, "and they have, consequently, no right to require me to do that which they themselves of right cannot."

Opposing the Tariff

In 1820, when the nation was suffering a depression (a period of poor economic conditions and high unemployment), a tariff bill was introduced into Congress. A tariff usually serves two important purposes. It can be used to raise some of the money needed to pay the expense of running the government. A tariff can also help new "infant" industries in a country compete against foreign products by taxing imported goods, thereby making them more costly than domestically manufactured goods.

In a speech before Congress, Tyler spoke against the tariff bill, arguing that manufacturing was not suffering any more than the farmer and needed no special consideration. He explained that the decline in sales of American goods abroad was due to the fact that the Napoleonic Wars in Europe were over and Europeans were now able to produce their own goods. If Americans continued to place a high tariff on their goods, Europeans would retaliate by refusing to buy American goods and America would lose the European market. By taxing imported goods, all Americans ended up paying more, since cheap European goods would no longer be available.

Tyler argued further that southern products, such as cotton and tobacco, had no tariff and sold well in a free market both in the United States and abroad. Most southerners, like Tyler, felt that the tariff bill favored northern industry and put the expense of the tariff on farmers, the majority of whom lived in the South and the West. To Tyler's delight, the Tariff Bill of 1820 was defeated – but the issue would plague Tyler right through his presidency.

SLAVE VERSUS FREE STATE

The tariff was not the only question being hotly debated in Congress in 1820. Another issue was what to do with the petition of the people of Missouri to become a state in the Union. As was customary when an area was seeking statehood, a bill was offered in the House of Representatives. Before any action could be taken, Representatives James Tallmadge of New York suddenly proposed an amendment which provided that no more slaves should be brought into Missouri and that "all children born within the said State, after the admission thereof into the Union, shall be free at the age of twenty-five years."

Since Maine was also seeking statehood that year, a compromise was proposed. Called the Missouri Compromise, Maine would be admitted as a "free" state and Missouri as a "slave" state. This would maintain the balance between the northern (free) and southern (slave) states. There was a precedent for this. The Northwest Ordinance of 1787 had stated that slavery would be prohibited in those states carved out of the Northwest Territory, the lands north of the Ohio River.

The Balance of Power

In a letter to a friend, Tyler expressed his concern. "You have no possible idea of the excitement that prevails here. Men talk of a dissolution of the Union with perfect nonchalance and indifference." It is obvious that as early as 1820, Tyler had serious concerns that the nation was dividing itself into two sections, each trying to maintain the balance of power.

In a brilliant speech on the Missouri Compromise, Tyler offered a rather unusual case in support of the expansion of slavery. If slavery were extended to new states, he argued, there would be less concentration of slaves in the old states. If there were less slaves in a state, the value of the slave would increase and in time, slavery would become too expensive to maintain. The abolition of slavery would come about naturally. Tyler's reasoning was widely accepted by southerners who were not only financially invested in slavery, but who feared what might occur if thousands of slaves were suddenly emancipated (freed).

With Congress in a deadlock over the problem of Missouri, a new amendment was proposed by Representative Jesse Thomas of Illinois. Missouri would be admitted to the Union without any restrictions on slavery, but slavery would be excluded from the rest of the Louisiana territory north of the 36°30′ parallel. Tyler voted against the Missouri Compromise and against every proposal to restrict slavery. The South gained Missouri as a slave state, but in the long run it lost the balance of power.

A Personal View of Slavery

How did Tyler view slavery, or what the North called "that peculiar institution"? Tyler was born into a household where slaves were a natural part of his childhood. He himself owned slaves all of his life. His advice to his overseers was to treat slaves well, because an unhappy slave was an unprofitable servant. Tyler felt that encouragement worked better than fear. He hated ever having to sell one of his slaves, and the sight of a slave auction could make him physically ill. He opposed the continuation of the slave trade from Africa, and as a U.S. senator, he promoted legislation to end slave auctions in Washington.

Yet, to the best of anyone's knowledge, Tyler never freed any of his slaves, as George Washington had done in his will. Nor did he offer or back any proposal for the abolition of slavery. There is no doubt that the economic welfare of Tyler's large family depended on the productivity of his plantation and the slave-labor system. He believed that slavery would die out through a form of "gradual abolition."

In 1838 Tyler was elected president of the Virginia Colonization Society. The group had been organized to support a plan to send blacks to Liberia, Africa, to form a new American colony there. It eased Tyler's conscience a bit to endorse the plan, but he was realistic enough to recognize that it was an impossible dream.

A LOW POINT IN LIFE

John Tyler was ill and discouraged. He had been suffering for several months from an illness, probably food poisoning. So in January 1821, he wrote a letter to the Richmond *Enquirer*, informing his constituents that he would not run for re-election, giving his illness as an excuse.

But it was more than illness that made 1821 such a difficult year. In a letter to a friend, Tyler explained, "The truth is, that I can no longer do good here. I stand in a decided minority, and to waste words on an obstinate majority is utterly useless and vain." He felt he was playing a losing battle against those who believed in a strong national government and loose construction of the Constitution. He also felt he would probably never go any higher in his political career.

Tyler brooded, too, about his financial position. A fourth baby was due that spring, and he wondered how he was going to be able to educate his children. While he was in Congress, he had limited time to attend to his law practice, and his income had fallen considerably during this period. For Tyler, it was a low point in his life.

Within a year, however, Tyler's fighting spirit revived. He was not only beginning to think about becoming involved in politics again, he felt well enough physically to become embroiled in a brawl with a hot-headed Virginia gentleman.

A Matter of Honor

Colonel John Mason, a witness in a lawsuit Tyler was contesting, felt that his honor had been insulted by Tyler's questions during a cross-examination. Meeting Tyler outside the courthouse later that day, the colonel accused Tyler of "taking liberties" with his reputation. Tyler's initial response was that he was not aware that he had offended the colonel. But when Mason retorted, "You, sir, have not acted the part of a gentleman," Tyler was enraged. Now it was *his* honor that was being attacked.

Tyler raised his arm and struck Mason with his fist. The colonel retaliated by striking Tyler with a riding whip. Tyler seized the whip and proceeded to slash Mason several times, ending the brawl. In describing the incident later, Tyler reported that he had escaped injury but that he had marked the colonel's face severely.

Obviously, Tyler's physical and emotional well-being was restored. When, in 1823, the people of his home county once more sought him out as a candidate for the Virginia House of Delegates, Tyler agreed to take another plunge into politics. This time, he would achieve higher office, but he would do battle with many men along the way.

Chapter 3

A Man of Principle

There were five men pursuing the presidency in 1824. Even in the Virginia House of Delegates, the presidential election created far more passion than any subject debated in the state legislature. Each candidate had his group of ardent supporters in the Virginia legislature. Each candidate was well known and four—Andrew Jackson, Henry Clay, John Calhoun, and John Quincy Adams—would leave their imprint on America's history. Moreover, it was a period in which the traditional method of electing the President was seriously being challenged.

Tyler had strong feelings about the five men seeking the presidency, and he was equally concerned about the Tennessee Resolution. This resolution was designed to destroy the caucus, the customary system whereby candidates in an election were selected by members of a political party at a closed meeting. Under the terms of the Tennessee Resolution, the people would be given a voice in the nominating process. Tyler opposed the idea because he knew that the presidential candidate who would profit most from a more democratic selection process would be Andrew Jackson. Tyler was relieved when the Tennessee Resolution did not pass in the Virginia legislature, but it was obvious that the undemocratic caucus system was on its way out.

THE PRESIDENTIAL CANDIDATES OF 1824

Jackson's appeal was to the illiterate frontiersmen and to those who admired his military adventures against the British and the Indians. While in the House of Representatives, Tyler had voted to censure Jackson for his invasion of Spanish Florida to attack the Seminole Indians and for his illegal execution of two pro-Seminole British citizens. Both incidents could have provoked war with Spain and Great Britain, nations which were, at that time, at peace with the United States. Tyler feared Jackson's unpredictable behavior and the way he had changed sides on major issues in order to be a popular candidate with the people.

Tyler was most unhappy when the states' rights candidate he favored, William Crawford, was stricken with a paralytic stroke. He could not bring himself to support either Henry Clay or John Calhoun, who were closely associated with a movement called the "American System."

Henry Clay and the American System

The American System was an idea that had been sponsored by Henry Clay since 1816. Clay believed that three things—a protective tariff, a national bank, and a government-supported system of internal improvements, such as road and canal building—would bind the nation more closely. He assumed that the tariff would protect new industries, increase the domestic market for consumer goods, and at the same time make the United States less dependent on goods from Europe. He hoped that the American System would make allies of the manufacturing interests of the North and the people of the West, who needed roads and canals for transporting goods in and out of the frontier areas.

In the period from 1816 to 1836, the country's growth and development may have required a moderate tariff and internal improvements, but the American System offered nothing to the South. To the states' rights advocates, such national undertakings meant a form of tyranny and taxation by a central government. They continued to argue that the Constitution gave no authority for such action and that the United States was a confederation of states, *not* a nation.

A Disastrous Election

The other presidential possibilities were John Calhoun and John Quincy Adams, son of the second President. Both men supported the American System. Tyler chose to back Adams, believing that once in office, he would be a more moderate and responsible President. Looking at the election as a reflection of the democratic process, the election was a disaster. Jackson won a plurality (the most number) of both the popular and electoral votes, but he did not have a majority, (more than half), of the electoral vote. In accordance with the Constitution, the election was thrown into the House of Representatives, where each state had one vote. Only the top three candidates could be considered. Adams and Crawford remained as possibilities and Clay, who came in fourth, was dropped. Clay advised his supporters to vote for Adams. When Crawford suffered a stroke and had to drop out, Adams, who had only 30% of the electoral and popular votes, became the sixth President. John Calhoun became Vice-President, and Adams selected Henry Clay to be his secretary of state. Jackson was out of the picture, but he would have his day four years later.

In the meantime, Tyler's star would begin to rise again. In 1825, just two years after returning to the Virginia legislature, he was elected to the highest position in the state, the governorship.

A man of great intelligence, John Calhoun's ideas on nullification and secession led indirectly to the Civil War. (Library of Congress.)

GOVERNOR OF VIRGINIA

The governor's mansion in which Tyler's father had lived had been replaced, and the new home offered much better surroundings to the Tyler family. But the role of governor had not changed from his father's time. Being governor of Virginia was a dignified and honored position, but it wielded little power and was more ceremonial than political. Under Virginia's first constitution, the governor was elected for a one-year term by both houses of the legislature. He had the right to suggest legislation to the assembly, but he had little power. He had no political party behind him to push for legislation he recommended, and he had no veto power (the right to prevent an act of Congress from becoming a law).

Tyler did recommend a system of public schools for all classes of people, but neither he nor the legislature was willing to fight for the higher taxes such a program would necessitate. He also suggested a road and canal program to bind the state, reminding the legislature that if the state did not help the western counties with such a program, the federal government would take over the job.

As Virginia's chief executive, Tyler also tried hard to convince the legislature that the salary of the governor did not adequately cover the social demands made upon him. The governor was expected to entertain the members of the legislature and their wives as well as the more important members of Richmond society. Letitia worked hard to provide simple but good fare at these official functions, but the expenses exceeded John's income. On one occasion, he attempted to make his point by inviting members of the legislature to a "banquet" at which he served only ham and large quantities of corn bread, washed down with cheap local whiskey. There is no record as to how well the home-style food was appreciated or whether the local brew made the lawmakers drunk, but his humorous effort did not succeed in getting the governor a raise in pay. By the time Tyler left office in January 1827, the family was in serious debt.

An Unexpected Run for the U.S. Senate

John Tyler's political career was a strange one. When he least campaigned for political office, good fortune would drop an offer in his lap. And he would win the office by being backed by political groups who opposed his stand on states' rights and nationalism. Such was the case with his election to the U.S. Senate in 1827. He had run for the office of senator in 1824 but had failed to win, though he had made a good showing. Now, suddenly, he had a second chance.

The incumbent senator was John Randolph, a brilliant advocate of states' rights who unfortunately had a biting tongue and some unusual manners. He once stated that Henry Clay reminded him "of a rotten mackerel lying in the sun and stinking." Randolph was reported to have strewn papers all over the Senate floor and refused to let anyone touch them. On another occasion, it was said he undressed and dressed himself in the Senate Chamber.

At this period in American history, U.S. senators were selected by their state legislatures. In January 1827, on the day before the members of the Virginia legislature were to vote for their choice of senator, a group of Randolph opponents approached Governor Tyler and asked permission to put up his name for the office. Tyler wavered between wanting to support Randolph for his political views and wanting to accept the nomination. His carefully worded statement sounded like a man who says no but really means yes. That was the interpretation of those who next day placed Tyler's name in nomination. When the vote was taken, Tyler won by a margin of five votes.

BACKING ANDREW JACKSON

Tyler returned to Washington just in time to become embroiled in the 1828 battle for the presidency. This time he would not back Adams, for he had been thoroughly disillusioned by the new President shortly after his first annual message to Congress. Adam's speech was dedicated to the principle of nationalism, calling for such actions as a federal program of internal improvements, a national university, a national militia law, and a national standard for weights and measures. Tyler was also worried that Adam's re-election would put his secretary of state, Henry Clay, next in line for the presidency.

Tyler preferred Governor DeWitt Clinton of New York, a man who had proved that internal improvements, like the Erie Canal, could be built with state funds, without federal support or interference. But when Clinton threw his support to Jackson in 1827, Tyler was left to choose between two candidates, neither of whom he could enthusiastically back: Adams or Jackson. Tyler chose Andrew Jackson. Just as he had done in 1824 with Adams, Tyler again based his decision on wishful thinking and rumors.

Deceiving Himself

Tyler had heard that, deep down, Jackson was a states' rights man and that the general's "ardent advocates from Tennessee are decidedly, as far as I can gather, in favor of limited construction of the Constitution." Tyler was not deceived by others in making his choice; he only deceived himself. Yet, he was far from happy with his decision.

In a letter to his brother-in-law, Dr. Henry Curtis, Tyler confessed, "Turning to [Jackson] I may at least indulge in hope, looking on Adams I must despair." The campaign was an ugly, mudslinging affair in which Tyler took no active part. With tens of thousands of newly franchised voters, the 1828 election of Jackson was a major democratic break with the past.

From Supporter to Opponent

As a well-bred southern gentleman, Tyler must have been appalled by the arrival of the drunken, fighting mobs of rough people who descended upon Washington for Jackson's inauguration. Aristocrats like Tyler were upset by the smell of whiskey on the new President's breath as he delivered his inauguration speech, and they were hardly impressed by the vague generalities expressed by their new leader.

Despite these events, Tyler's relations with Jackson were still good. Following an invitation to the White House for dinner, Tyler noted how impressed he had been with Jackson's old-fashioned good manners. "He [Jackson] even went so far as to introduce his guests to one another—a thing without precedent here and most abominably unfashionable."

Tyler also was pleased when Jackson vetoed the controversial Maysville Road Bill. Jackson turned it down on the basis that because it was being built totally within the state of Kentucky, it was not an interstate road and therefore did not qualify for federal funds. Tyler and the strict constructionists were also heartened by Jackson's veto of the renewal of the charter for the Bank of the United States, which Clay tried to push through Congress in 1832.

It did not take long, however, for the southern aristocrats to realize that the goal of Jackson and his cronies was to break the hold of the moneyed and privileged class. The first inkling that Tyler and his friends had about the changes in the old order was Jackson's open avowal of the so-called "spoils system." Although other Presidents, from Thomas Jefferson on, had used the power of patronage (political appointments to gain party support), none had done it quite so openly as Jackson. He fired civil service appointees who had been friendly to the Adams administration or who threatened to sabotage his policies.

Tyler also saw Jackson's appointment of newspapermen to public office as a threat to a free press. At a time when the only way that the average man could learn about the workings of the government was through the newspapers, Tyler had a right to be concerned. However, he failed to take into account that many of the newspapers were owned by wealthy men whose opposition to Jackson was openly expressed in *their* newspapers.

Recess Appointments

Tyler was equally concerned about Jackson's use of recess appointments to put his political choices into office. By assigning people to diplomatic positions while Congress was recessed, Jackson got around the constitutional mandate that such presidential appointments were to be made by the "advice and consent" of the Senate. Jackson argued that the business of government had to go on whether Congress was in session or not and that debating the appointments afterwards was a waste of time.

Such a flagrant abuse of the Constitution brought out Tyler's best oratory. In a speech before the Senate in February 1831, he attacked Jackson. "There is already enough of the spice of monarchy in the presidential office. . . . There lies the true danger to our institutions. . . . Place in the President's hands . . . the uncontrolled power of appointing to office and liberty cannot abide among us." Tyler was gratified to find that a majority of the Senate agreed with him.

Calhoun Breaks with Jackson

John Calhoun's place on the Democratic ticket as the vice-presidential candidate had helped gain southern support for Jackson's election in 1828. But by 1831, Calhoun and President Jackson were barely speaking to each other. Calhoun, the passionate states' rights advocate, had written a pamphlet in which he argued that since a state was a member of a *voluntary* compact of states, it had the right to nullify or refuse to accept any federal law that the state decided was unconstitutional. This principle of "nullification" would become the basis of South Carolina's threat to secede (leave) from the Union in 1832 and bring the nation to the brink of civil war.

The Men Who Would Be President

From the end of Andrew Jackson's administration to the election of Abraham Lincoln, a period of almost 25 years, the country was led by Presidents who lacked broad intellectual powers or strong personalities. Tyler tried to assert himself by the use of the veto, just as Jackson had done, but Tyler did not have the confidence of his party or the public image and support of the populace that Jackson had cultivated so successfully.

The political vacuum from 1837 to 1850 was filled by three strong congressional figures, Daniel Webster, Henry Clay, and John C. Calhoun. Each of them fought zealously for the presidency. Each of them failed. Yet they succeeded in transforming the Senate into a forum for silver-tongued orators and fresh ideas, powerful enough to thwart the efforts of the President of the United States. During these years, the personalities and the words of these three men left more of an imprint on the period than did the efforts of those who did attain the White House. And each of them played an important role in the presidency of John Tyler.

All three men were lawyers, and all three were among the foremost orators of their day. Webster was a graduate of Dartmouth College; Calhoun, a graduate of Yale. Clay lacked formal schooling but attracted as his mentor the first professor of law in the new nation, George Wythe. Each of the men served both in the House of Representatives and in the Senate. Though none of the three attained the presidency, each served in the executive as well as the legislative branch of the government. Each was secretary of state in a presidential cabinet, and John Calhoun was Vice-President under both John Quincy Adams and Andrew Jackson. Each of them joined the Whig Party, and both Clay and Webster played an important role in the development and death of that party.

Each man represented a particular section of the country. Webster, originally from New Hampshire, represented mainly the business interests of the rising industrial and mercantile class of the North. Calhoun, from South Carolina, represented the South, particularly southern planters. Henry Clay was a native-born Virginian whose family had migrated to Kentucky when he was 15 years old. "Harry of the West" came to represent the interests of the new territories being opened along the western frontier.

In their early careers, Clay and Calhoun were ardent nationalists. During the War of 1812, there was no greater "War Hawk" than Henry Clay. Calhoun and Webster first debated each other in the House of Representatives, Calhoun justifying the war, Webster opposing it.

Initially, Calhoun and Clay also favored a protective tariff. Webster, as a spokesman for the New England mercantile and shipping community, began as a believer in the strict "delegated and limited" powers of the Con-

stitution. The protective tariff was not a
power given to Congress, according to Webster. Later, as the interests of those he
represented changed, so did his ideas on the
subject. In 1827, when the British began
dumping woolen goods on the American market at prices that threatened to close New England woolen mills, Webster's loyalty to his
constituents pushed him into voting for the
passage of the Tariff Bill of 1828.

As their careers progressed, Calhoun
would give up being a nationalist and would
become a passionate states' rights advocate.
Webster would become the spokesman for
nationalism and the need for a strong federal
government. Clay would remain consistent in
maintaining his stand on the need for a strong
national government. His "American System"
called for a planned national economy, with a
national bank, a protective tariff, and federally
improved roads and canals that would link the
nation together.

By the end of the War of 1812, the Feder-
alist Party was dying. The Republican Party,
which had begun as an opponent to the Fed-
eralists, now developed into two camps, the
National Republicans, with Clay as one of its
leaders, and the Democratic-Republicans,
which became, under Jackson, the Democratic Party.

As early as 1824, Clay and Calhoun were
contenders for the White House. But when
the election results produced no presidential
candidate with a majority of votes, the

decision was given to the House of Representatives. Only the top three candidates were
considered. Since Clay came in fourth, he
was faced with a choice of giving his votes
to either John Quincy Adams or Andrew
Jackson. Clay threw his support to Adams
and ended up as secretary of state. Calhoun
became Vice-President. Four years later, Calhoun also served as Vice-President under Andrew Jackson.

In the decades following 1830, two political parties evolved that were to organize
American political life in a new way. By the
election of 1832, a definite split had erupted
in what had been the Democratic-Republican
Party. Those who opposed the arrogant taking of power by President Andrew Jackson
came from many sources. One source was
the National Republicans, the first group of
anti-Jacksonites. Eventually, a party called
the Whigs evolved out of the ashes of the
National Republican Party. It was composed
of such diverse groups as nationalists and
those who believed in states' rights, Northern
industrialists and southern planters, and those
who believed in the protective tariff and
those who despised it. The only cement bind-
ing the Whigs together was a mutual distrust
of Jackson. It was led by the "Big Three"—
Webster, Clay, and Calhoun—all men still in
their prime.

In 1833 Clay, Calhoun, and Webster
united in their oratorical skills to pass the
resolution that censured Jackson for daring to

force the removal of government deposits from the Bank of the United States. But when it came time in 1836 for the Whig Party to put forth its first candidate for the White House, the three men were shunted aside for General William Henry Harrison as President and John Tyler as Vice-President. Though the Whigs lost the election, the strong showing by their candidates was encouraging to the party.

Calhoun died in 1850. Clay and Webster would die two years later. Webster would have one more opportunity for the presidency, in 1852, but he would lose the nomination to General Winfield Scott. That seemed to be the final blow to the tired Webster, for he died shortly thereafter.

Tyler, whose political life had been so affected by the three men, would be the only one to survive to witness the beginning of the Civil War, which had threatened for so long. When the war finally came, it would be Webster's words on the need for maintaining the Union that would be adopted by Lincoln in several of his speeches.

JACKSON RE-ELECTED

The man who maneuvered himself into the vice-presidency on the Democratic ticket in 1832 was Martin Van Buren, champion of the common man in New York State. His efforts helped to bring about an alliance of farmers along the western frontier and workers in the growing cities along the East

Coast. With Henry Clay running on the Republican ticket, Tyler was forced to choose between the lesser of two evils and again threw his weight to Jackson. With Van Buren as his running mate, Jackson won a smashing victory with which to begin his second term in office.

At a state convention called immediately after the election, South Carolina officially nullified (cancelled) two federal tariff bills that had been passed in 1828 and 1832. South Carolina also threatened secession if the federal government attempted to force the state to collect the tariffs. Calhoun resigned from the vice-presidency in December of 1832 and took a seat in the Senate, which was available because the former senator had been selected to be the state governor. Once in the Senate, Calhoun launched a campaign against the tariffs, using his idea of nullification as the basis for South Carolina's refusal to accept the legislation.

IN A BIND

President Jackson wasted no time in declaring the whole idea of nullification absurd. He argued that the federal government was indivisible, and for a state to withdraw from the Union would be treason. The President threatened to use force to compel South Carolina to comply with the law and asked Congress to give him the power by passing the so-called "Force Bill." This authorized the President to use the army and navy, if necessary, to enforce the law. In his annual message to Congress, Jackson did hold out an olive branch to South Carolina by recommending that tariffs be lowered.

The situation put Tyler in a terrible bind. He believed that as long as a state remained within the Union, it did not have the right to nullify federal laws. On the other hand, he opposed the tariffs, and he held that the principle of states' rights gave a state the right to secede. Tyler also held that the Force Bill was unconstitutional, that Jackson had "swept away the barriers of the Constitution and given us in place of the Federal government, under which we fondly believed we were living, a consolidated military despotism."

To avoid the bloody consequences if the Force Bill passed, Tyler sought to find a compromise. He worked behind the scenes, urging Clay, a supporter of the bill, to meet with Calhoun and try to work out an agreement that would satisfy both sides. Because neither side truly wanted a civil war, an agreement was reached in a few weeks. When Clay announced on February 11, 1833, that he would introduce a compromise tariff bill, Tyler later said, "I recall the enthusiasm I felt that day when Mr. Clay rose in the Senate to announce the great measure of peace and reconciliation. I occupied the extreme seat on the left; he a similar one on the right of the Senate chamber. We advanced to meet each other, and grasped each other's hands midway the chamber."

Re-elected to the Senate

The crisis over the tariff was over, but not Tyler's concern about the issues involved in the Force Bill. He was up for re-election and his actions would be closely watched. His southern colleagues had dropped their opposition to the bill and he risked much by his opposition. But on February 6, Tyler made a stinging attack on the measure. When the vote was taken on February 20, John Tyler's was the lone "Nay" vote. For Tyler, it was a matter of principle. The idea of the Force Bill was unconstitutional, it could lead to bloodshed, and he would *not* vote for it. Nine days after his brilliant speech, the Virginia legislature re-elected him on the first ballot by a majority of only one vote.

But the President and the Democratic Party, which expected greater loyalty from its members, were not as forgiving. Tyler's open defiance of Jackson's policy would soon create a break with the President, and he would find himself allied with the antiadministration forces.

Chapter 4

A Break with "King Andrew"

John Tyler was a doting father. In the nine years he spent as a senator in Washington, he wrote long and loving letters to Letitia and the children. Those years may have been politically rewarding, but they kept him away from his family for long periods of time. Much of what we know about Tyler's personal life comes from the letters he wrote to his wife and children while he was living in Washington.

By 1830, the Tylers were the proud parents of seven children. One, sickly little Anne Contesse, died at the age of three months. Tyler found it hard to be away from his family, and the long and loving letters he wrote to his children reveal affection, concern for their welfare, and much fatherly advice.

To his oldest daughter, Mary, pretty and much admired when she visited Washington with her mother, he wrote, "Without intellectual improvement, the most beautiful of the sex is but a figure of wax works." To his second son, John, who turned out to be the most rebellious, he wrote, "Have *hours* for reading and *minutes* for playing and you will be a clever fellow." He urged his children to have good manners and to take advantage of their education. The education of his daughters was no less important than the education of his sons. Knowing this, his second daughter, Letitia, in a letter to her father, wisely combined a request to attend a ball in

Williamsburg with assurances that she was doing well in her philosophy and chemistry studies.

STRICT VIEWS

In an age when a man was expected to both dominate and protect the females in his family, John Tyler followed the customs rigidly. He held strict views about what was proper behavior for young men and women. He was shocked when he first saw the waltz being danced and in a letter to his 12-year-old daughter, he described it as "a dance which you have never seen, and which I do not desire to see you dance. It is rather vulgar, I think." He would later change his mind when the second Mrs. Tyler introduced waltzing into the White House.

From an early age, Tyler's children were made aware of the great political issues of the day. He wanted them to know about the world in which he worked and they lived, and he took the time to patiently explain what was going on. He would write about major occurrences of the day and never fail to explain his own decisions on issues. No wonder the Tyler children became strong advocates of states' rights.

Despite his high expectations of his children and the shortage of money with which he constantly seemed to live, Tyler seemed to find funds to indulge his offspring when necessary. He sent his sons extra spending money so they could attend dances and balls at college and enjoy collegiate social life, and he provided Mary with an elaborate wedding, which he really could not afford.

A good part of Tyler's money problems lay in the poor management of his funds. It only took an urgent request from a relative or friend for Tyler to give the person a loan. Often he would borrow on his own property in order to offer the loan. Like many Virginia planters, he was land-rich, but often short of cash.

THE BANK ISSUE AGAIN

With the Compromise Tariff Bill passed and the nullification crisis over, the lone dissenter of the Force Bill returned in triumph to Virginia. A dinner was held in Tyler's honor. In the speech he delivered that evening, Tyler reminded his audience that he did not approve of South Carolina's actions on nullification; rather, he had objected to Jackson's threat of using armed force. In an impassioned delivery, Tyler called Jackson's action a threat of "military dictatorship."

Such words were propelling Tyler into the anti-Jackson camp, led by none other than Henry Clay. Once again, choosing between what he saw as two evils, Tyler now praised Clay as the statesman who had "rescued us from civil war, when those who held or ought to have held our destinies in their hands talked of swords and halters." Tyler's fiery statements were bringing him to the brink of a total break with Jackson and the Democratic Party.

The event which finally sent Tyler into the arms of Jackson's enemies centered around the Bank of the United States. In the 1832 presidential campaign, the Republicans selected the bank issue as the one that would mobilize the party and bring the American people to their side. Though the bank was not due to come up for recharter until 1836, the Republicans pressed for an immediate 15-year extension in 1832. Although the recharter bill was passed by both houses of Congress, Jackson promptly vetoed the measure. Still a Democrat and an opponent of the bank, as was Virginia and most of the South, Tyler voted against the recharter bill and also voted to sustain Jackson's veto.

Destroying the Bank

Despite Congress' support of the bank, Jackson saw his own victory in the 1832 election as a mandate (order) from the common people to abolish the bank once and for all. What

Jackson decided to do was to remove all government deposits from the Bank of the United States, thereby destroying it before its official end in 1836.

In order to do this, Jackson had to find a secretary of the treasury who would go along with his plans. He juggled several secretaries of the treasury until he finally transferred his attorney general, Roger B. Taney, to the position of secretary of the treasury. Taney not only believed in the legality of Jackson's stand but he was willing to sign the order for the removal of government funds from the federal bank to 23 state banks. All of this took place while Congress was in recess and could not interfere with Jackson's actions.

When Congress convened in December 1833, the bank problem became the main issue between the two political parties. Regular Democrats stood steadfastly behind Jackson's determination to crush the bank; Republicans had become its most ardent supporters. Allied with the Republicans were former Democrats who had been drummed out of the party for failing to support Jackson and his views.

On the day after Christmas, Henry Clay began his attack on Jackson with a two-day speech, calling for action on two resolutions, censuring (condemning) both Jackson and Taney. The first resolution charged both men with illegally removing deposits from the federal bank. The second and more important charge was that "the President, in the late Executive proceedings in relation to the public revenue, has assumed upon himself authority and power not conferred by the Constitution and laws, but in derogation of both." Among those backing Clay's resolutions were Webster and Calhoun.

JOINING THE OPPOSITION

Tyler was in a quandary. Should he vote for restoration of the funds or not? Should he vote for the censuring of Jackson? If those who supported the bank would agree not to seek a

The presidency of Andrew Jackson marked a dramatic increase in the participation of the common man in American government. Voting rights were extended to a much larger segment of the population, and for the first time, presidential candidates were nominated at national conventions instead of closed state legislative conferences. (Library of Congress.)

new charter, the funds could be restored and gradually withdrawn without any great shock to the nation's economy. But if the probank Democrats were out to win a new charter, restoring the deposits would strengthen the bank and add to the power of the moneyed aristocracy. It was probably Tyler's distrust of "King Andrew" Jackson's intentions more than anything else which made him throw his support to Clay's resolutions. The Senate debate was to last three months.

Once his decision was made, Tyler became a prominent leader of the anti-Jackson forces, and when he finally rose to speak on February 24, 1834, the Senate chamber was filled to capacity. Tyler first dealt with the bank. As he saw it, the establishment of the bank had always been an unconstitutional act, and he had always wanted it to die. The only question was *how* the bank should die. "I say, if it is to die, let it die by law. . . . If the President had rested on his veto, the Bank was dead." Tyler then proceeded to attack Jackson's removal of the federal deposits. "Sir, give the President control over the purse – the power to place the immense revenues of the country into any hands he may please, and I care not what you call him, he is 'every inch a king.' "

Birth of the Whigs

It was obvious during the long speech that Tyler had now made a definite break with the Democratic-Republican Party (or, as it had become known during the Jackson era, simply the Democratic Party). He was now openly allied with a new party being formed under the leadership of Henry Clay, John C. Calhoun, and Daniel Webster. The new party was called the Whigs, after the British party which had worked to reduce the authority of the king and to give more power to Parliament. But Tyler was to prove as difficult a party member for the Whigs as he had been for the Democrats. A streak of independence and old-fashioned morality would continue to make Tyler vote his conscience rather than the party line.

Tyler was now convinced that Jackson's star was fading. When the Virginia General Assembly instructed its U.S. senators to vote for censure of Jackson, Tyler was sure that America was getting over its love affair with Jacksonian democracy and its popular appeal to the masses. But Tyler would soon be forced to realize that after Jackson, American politics would never be the same.

A Prospective Candidate

The censure issue would not die. On the very day that the condemnation of Jackson was passed, Senator Thomas Hart Benton of Missouri, the leading Democrat in the Senate, swore publicly that he would not rest until the censure resolution had been erased from the *Congressional Journal*, the formal minutes of the proceedings of Congress. Tyler, of course, had voted for the censure of Jackson.

If Benton had been angry when Tyler voted for censure, he was now more irate than ever when John Tyler was chosen to head another congressional committee to investigate the bank. The committee was stacked four to one against the Jackson administration. Nevertheless, its final report was well documented and reasonably fair, and in the end it tended to be favorable to the bank and its president, Nicholas Biddle.

Benton, however, saw the report as an attack on Jackson, Secretary of the Treasury Taney, and himself. He called the criticisms, "False! False as hell!" But some of the Whigs thought otherwise. Tyler had never favored a federal bank, but his pro-Biddle report during the investigation made some Whigs feel that Tyler's moderation on the issue might make him a good vice-presidential candidate on the Whig ticket in 1836. The Democrats who now controlled the Virginia House of Delegates had other ideas.

FACING A DILEMMA

These Democrats were now determined to get Tyler out of the Senate. The device they used was an order to the two Virginia senators, Tyler and Benjamin W. Leigh, to vote for Benton's newest resolution to expunge (erase) the censuring of Jackson from the *Congressional Journal.*

The decision now before Tyler was a perilous one, for it involved his personal finances, his political career, and his honor. He loved his role in the Senate, and he needed the Senate salary to pay his mounting expenses. Some of his friends urged him to resign and held out offers of a judgeship. But Tyler would not listen to their pleas.

Defying Instructions

Despite the order given by the Virginia House of Delegates, Leigh decided to vote against the resolution but to remain in the Senate. But Tyler could not in all conscience do so. If he gave in to the Democrats and voted for the expunging resolution, he would be supporting an action that he believed was unconstitutional. And if he did not vote for it, he would be defying the instructions of the Virginia legislature.

How could he vote against the legislature's instructions when, during his very first days in the Virginia House of Delegates in 1811, he had spoken out against senators who defied the mandate of the state legislature which had elected them? Tyler could have taken the position that his words in 1811 were those of a young and inexperienced man, and that he now had a more mature outlook on the subject of instructions. But that was not in keeping with his character. He was a man of principles, not a practical politician, and once attached to a principle, he would not, or could not, change his mind. This element of Tyler's character would persist throughout his life and be the cause of many of his political problems.

The Whig leadership did not want to lose such a prominent member, and they sent Calhoun and Clay to urge Tyler to keep his seat in the Senate. But the two persuasive and practical politicians failed to influence Tyler's decision. After listening to Tyler, an incredulous Calhoun said, "If you make it a point of personal honor, we have nothing more to say." Tyler's mind was made up.

In February 1836, when the Virginia Assembly passed what Tyler called the "villainous instructions," he resigned his Senate seat. The Virginia legislature promptly selected William C. Rives to fill Tyler's unexpired term. When the Benton resolution came up for a vote in January 1837, Rives, as expected, voted for expunging the censure of Jackson. With the Democrats in control, the measure passed in the Senate. Benton's perseverance had at last paid off.

Return to Gloucester Farm

Back home in Virginia, the Whigs and anti-Jackson forces were unsure how to deal with both Tyler and Leigh. Tyler had been courageous in resigning rather than giving up his principles; Leigh had been equally brave in remaining in the Senate to continue his fight against the pro-Jackson faction. The Whigs finally decided to hold a dinner in Richmond to honor both men. Needless to say, the evening was strained and at times embarrassing as the guests tried to pay homage to two men who had taken two such different roads. The Richmond *Enquirer* could not help ridiculing the situation.

After eight years in Washington, Tyler looked forward to joining his wife and children at Gloucester Farm, an estate in Charles City County that he had purchased in 1829. But the years in the Senate had done much damage to the family finances. Tyler's personal affairs were in such "utter disorder" that he soon sold the farm and moved his family to Williamsburg so that he could once more resume his law practice. But he would not be out of public life for long. The Whigs had plans for him.

Chapter 5

From Democrat to Whig

Tyler's political career, from the beginning of the Jackson era to the end of his own administration as President, spanned some remarkable changes in American government. During those years, 1828–1844, the people of the United States witnessed three important events. The first was a movement towards giving the common man greater participation in his government, a movement called "Jacksonian democracy."

RISE OF THE COMMON MAN

The United States had always offered an opportunity for men to rise above lowly beginnings. But the Jackson era celebrated the common man. Jackson's election marked the end of the Virginia dynasty Presidents, all of whom had come from aristocratic families. Now public affairs were no longer the business of gentlemen from old and distinguished families. The westward movement had begun, and life on the frontier and the need for cooperative effort fostered equality.

The constitutions of the new western states gave the vote to all male taxpayers, not only to men of property. Gradually, the eastern states were also enacting more liberal voting requirements. The difference in the number of voters between the presidential elections of 1824 and 1828 proves the point dramatically. In 1828, 56 percent of adult white males voted, more than twice the number that voted in 1824. By the election of 1840, 78 percent of the white male population voted, though secret ballots were still not used. In addition, the caucus system, in which candidates were nominated in secret sessions of the state legislatures, gave way to national nominating conventions.

The second important event involved a great power struggle — a tug-of-war between the President and Congress. Before the Jackson era, Presidents had rarely used the veto to thwart the power of the legislative branch of the government for fear of arousing violent opposition from Congress. But both Jackson and Tyler dared to effectively employ the veto in their stuggle for supremacy.

Rise of Political Parties

The third change was the development of political parties as we know them today. As late as 1820, President Monroe was re-elected without opposition. But after 1824, when the presidential election was decided in the House of Representatives, a true party system began to develop.

Originally, what came to be known as the Whig Party was really not a political party at all. It had no platform and no underlying principles. The only glue holding the various Whig factions together was a hatred of President Jackson and his successor, President Martin Van Buren, and a common concern about the growth of a new popular democracy. Two major groups, with totally opposing agendas, made up the largest segments of the party.

One group, the National Republicans, was led by Henry

As Speaker of the U.S. House of Representatives, Henry Clay changed the position from a mere presiding officer to one of power and prestige. As a U.S. senator, he dared to challenge the authority of both Presidents William Henry Harrison and John Tyler. (Library of Congress.)

Clay and Daniel Webster. They represented the merchants, shippers, and the new industrialists in the Northeast. They opposed slavery and believed in a loose interpretation of the Constitution. They supported the Bank of the United States, the protective tariff, and internal improvements—ideas all favorable to the growing class of businessmen.

The other powerful Whig group was led by John Calhoun, Judge Hugh L. White of Tennessee—and John Tyler. They were former Democrats who were also disenchanted with Jackson. They represented the South and the interests of the slaveholding plantation owners. They believed in free trade, strict construction of the Constitution, and the doctrine of states' rights.

Other, less powerful Whig groups included conservative Democrats in Pennsylvania, New York, and Ohio who were disgusted with Van Buren and his political machine. They were also fearful of the radical ideas of a group of urban workers known in New York as Locofocos.

THE ELECTION OF 1836

How were the Whigs going to toss all these different elements into the same pot and produce a stew good enough to serve to the American public and win an election? Tyler suggested that the Whig presidential candidate in 1836 be someone who could unite the South and not be offensive to anti-Van Buren Democrats and National Republicans in the North. Others favored having state legislatures and state nominating conventions select regional candidates. These Whigs hoped to repeat the election of 1824, when no candidate received a majority of electoral votes and the election was thrown into the House of Representatives. The dream was that this time the House would then choose one of the Whig nominees.

Three Candidates

With this idea in mind, the Whigs selected three presidential candidates. To satisfy the North and the National Republicans in that territory, Daniel Webster, a senator from Massachusetts, was chosen. Judge Hugh White was nominated to appeal to the states' rights group and the South's anti-Jackson group. The man chosen in order to obtain the western vote was General William Henry Harrison, a Virginia-born Ohioan.

The success of Andrew Jackson, presented to the American public as "Old Hickory," a war hero and frontier fighter, prodded the Whigs to do likewise. Although he was a mediocre soldier, Harrison had won a victory over the Indians at the Battle of Tippecanoe in Indiana. He had been governor of the Indiana Territory, an Ohio state senator, and a member of both Houses of Congress. But he supported no burning issues, and the best that could be said for him was that he could speak at great length on all sides of a subject and say nothing. Indeed, he himself admitted to a friend, "I have news more strange to tell you. Some folks are silly enough to have formed a plan to make a President of the United States out of this *clerk* and Clodhopper!"

A Sit-Back-and-Wait Candidate

It is ironic that on the very same day that the Virginia Whigs nominated Tyler to be Vice-President, his state legislature passed the resolution whose instructions forced Tyler's resignation from the U.S. Senate. Though Tyler did nothing to encourage or discourage the idea, his name was put into nomination in several states. The Virginia Whigs offered him on a White–Tyler ticket, but when the western part of the state demanded Harrison, a second convention was held and a Har-

rison–Tyler ticket was also offered. It was agreed that which-
ever candidate, Harrison or White, got the majority of votes,
the state electors would give all their votes to that candidate.
Such shenanigans could not help but produce confusion—
and it did.

Hoping to repeat the success of Andrew Jackson's campaign as a frontiersman and soldier, Harrison's political
managers built up the image of their candidate as an Indian
fighter and as a hero of the War of 1812 against the British
in hopes that this would bring voters in the West to the Whig
ranks. The Whig campaign slogan was "Tippecanoe and Tyler,
too." It was intended to remind voters of Harrison's deeds as
an Indian fighter at Tippecanoe River in Indiana.

Once nominated, Tyler did nothing to win the office.
Though urged by his friends to go to "every man's house, talk
to him as tho' everything was in his power—flatter the wife
and daughters and praise the hogs," Tyler would not campaign.
He preferred sitting on the porch in his Williamsburg home
to kissing babies, flattering politicians, or making political
statements.

Selecting a Vice-President

The Democrats ran Van Buren with Colonel Richard M. Johnson of Kentucky for the vice-presidency. The Whig strategy
failed. Van Buren easily won a majority of the votes, with
Harrison garnering almost twice as many Whig votes as White
and Webster combined. But for the first and only time in
American history, the Senate was forced to decide the election of the Vice-President (at that time, Presidents and Vice-
Presidents were elected separately). Colonel Johnson, though
far in the lead with 147 electoral votes, lacked one vote for
a majority. Granger had 77 votes and Tyler had 47. Since
the Democrats controlled the Senate, Johnson was chosen.

The election results did not dampen Tyler's spirits for long. He had become better known throughout the nation, and he had run for office without having to compromise his states' rights ideals. Besides, the next few years afforded Tyler an opportunity to be home with his family and to rebuild his faltering law practice.

FAMILY UPS-AND-DOWNS

In the years between 1836–1840, the Tyler children began to marry and produce grandchildren. Sadly, several of his children's marriages failed miserably. But one was a source of great joy to Tyler. That was the marriage of his son, Robert, to Priscilla Cooper of Bristol, Pennsylvania. What was unusual about this marriage in such an aristocratic family as John Tyler's was the fact that Priscilla was an actress – in those days a lowly occupation on the social scale.

Though descended on her mother's side from a Chief Justice of the New York Supreme Court, Priscilla's father, Thomas Cooper, was a well-known actor – and a gambler and a drinker as well. When her mother died when Priscilla was 18 years old, the affairs and finances of the Cooper family were in desperate shape. Her father's acting reputation had long since faded, and there was no other income to care for the many Cooper children. Priscilla saw no alternative but to become an actress.

Coached by her father, Priscilla soon found work on the stage. Though pretty and hardworking, she was not very talented. For three years, Priscilla and her father acted in second-rate theaters and lived in grimy boardinghouses, and then the Depression of 1837 hit. With the country facing difficult financial problems and unemployment, the people had little money to waste on such frivolous pleasures as the theater.

Romance in Richmond

In a letter to her sister on March 18, 1837, Priscilla confessed that if someone "with a large establishment in Virginia, a good family name, and a handsome and good-natured person" were to ask her hand in marriage, she would consider such a proposal not "to be sneezed at." That was the very same day that Priscilla and Tom Cooper reached Richmond, Virginia, to appear in Shakespeare's *Othello*. In the audience was Robert Tyler, who had been studying law in a Williamsburg law office and had been lured to Richmond for the evening by the idea of seeing a Shakespeare play.

When Priscilla appeared on stage as the beautiful Desdemona, the audience gave her a standing ovation, a southern gesture of respect often paid to young and pretty actresses. Robert was so taken by Priscilla's beauty that he found himself standing long after the rest of the audience was seated.

By the time the play was over, Robert Tyler was completely smitten. He dashed backstage, sought out Thomas Cooper, and asked permission to "pay his addresses" to Priscilla. It took over a year and a half, six proposals, and dozens of love letters before Priscilla finally consented to be Robert's wife. John Tyler must have approved of his son's choice, because he was best man at the wedding.

Priscilla Cooper Tyler was a welcome addition to the Tyler clan. She was solicitous and loving to her husband's mother, Letitia, who had been ailing for some time. She was happy and helpful — and careful with money, a quality lacking in much of the Tyler family. And she was soon to take an active role in her father-in-law's political career.

NEW FRIENDS AND OLD PLANS

Tyler was now securely seated in the ranks of the Whig Party. But this must have been embarrassing to him for it was obvious that the Whig Party was more and more becoming a spokesman for all that Tyler deplored — nationalism, the protective tariff, and internal improvements. Seeing the direction in which the Whigs were moving had forced John Calhoun and other prominent southerners to return to the Democratic fold.

Tyler, however, remained loyal to his new friends. Being addicted to politics, he was once more making plans for his return to the political arena. In April 1838, he ran as a Whig for the Virginia House of Delegates from the Williamsburg district and was promptly swept into office for his third term of service. A year later, he was elected Speaker of the Virginia Assembly.

But Tyler really had his heart set on returning to Washington. It looked as if Henry Clay would be the Whig candidate for President in 1840, and if so, Tyler knew he had no chance for the vice-presidency. Clay, a Kentuckian, would need someone outside of the South in order to balance the ticket. What Tyler wanted was the Senate seat that he had resigned in February 1836.

Backstage Manipulations

William C. Rives, who had succeeded Tyler in the Senate, had been elected as a Jackson Democrat. But Rives had broken with the Jackson–Van Buren group and was now calling himself a Conservative Democrat. Though they had split with Van Buren in 1838, the Conservative Democrats had not yet allied themselves with the Whigs. Clay and other Whig leaders wanted Rives and his friends in the Whig ranks. Virginia was an important state in a presidential election, and Clay wanted all the support he could gather in the 1840 presidential race. Quietly working behind the scenes, Clay let it be known that he was backing Rives in the coming Rives–Tyler contest.

Tyler found it hard to believe that any Whig would vote for a man who so recently had been a Jackson–Van Buren supporter. When the first ballots were counted in the Virginia legislature, Rives had 29 votes to Tyler's 62 and 68 for the Democratic candidate, John Y. Mason. As the balloting continued, Tyler saw his votes declining and Rives increasing. He began to suspect that someone was pulling strings behind the scene.

Henry Wise, Tyler's good friend in Washington, was asked to meet with Clay. In a stormy session, Clay admitted that though he preferred Tyler, he felt Rives had a better chance to capture the state. Clay offered to have Whig leaders nominate Tyler for the vice-presidency on the Whig ticket if he would release his votes to secure Rives' election.

Tyler refused the out and out bribe. As a result, the election was stalemated. Much of the state's business was put aside as the balloting continued, and many a Whig felt less than pleased with Tyler's stubborn stand. That stand would cost him votes in the 1840 election. In February 1839, the assembly decided to postpone the election indefinitely. Virginia was left with one representative in the United States Senate. It was not until January 1841, after 29 roll calls, that the deadlocked election was finally decided in favor of Rives. But by that time Tyler had already been nominated and elected to be the next Vice-President of the United States.

Chapter 6

Tippecanoe and Tyler, Too

For pure hokum, the election campaign of 1840 has never been surpassed. Both parties stooped to low levels of electioneering. Compared to the antics of the Whigs, the Democratic campaign seemed almost dignified. The Whig strategy was born out of a desire to outdo Jackson's campaign appeal to the common man. It was helped tremendously by an economic depression that much of the public blamed on the incumbent Democratic President, Martin Van Buren. In truth, however, the depression had its roots in the Jackson era.

THE PANIC OF 1837

The sale of public lands in the West in the years after 1820 had opened new frontiers. As roads and canals were constructed to link the East with the new territories in the West, hundreds of thousands of settlers began to migrate westward to buy government land and settle along the frontier as farmers.

But the offering of government lands also proved irresistible to speculators. The same plots were often sold and resold several times without once being held by anyone who expected to farm it. From 1834 to 1836, government land sales increased from four million dollars to 24 million dollars. These funds were deposited in Jackson's "pet banks" (state banks that had been selected to receive government deposits), which often made loans to speculators to buy and sell land again.

The Beginning of a Depression

To stop the land speculation, Jackson ordered Secretary of the Treasury Levi Woodbury to issue a "Specie Circular." The circular stated that all purchases of public lands had to be made in "specie"–that is, bought with gold or silver coins. Paper currency would no longer be acceptable. Jackson was careful to see that the order did not go into effect until after the election of 1836. State banks had little hard money (gold or silver coins) available to back their loans. Speculators could no longer pay for land with paper currency and banks could no longer afford to make risky loans. Land values began to plummet. Speculation in land had been halted, but the decline in prices began to snowball, marking the beginning of a depression.

However, money collected from the protective tariffs as well as the sale of government land had created a surplus in the national treasury. Jackson asked Congress to distribute the surplus to the states as loans. But individual states and private businessmen had already borrowed funds from foreign investors for internal improvements. While prosperity existed, the states and private investors had extended themselves and stretched their borrowing capacity to the limit. When worried foreign investors began to call for payment in gold or silver, the state banks found themselves unable to repay the loans. The real panic began in May 1837, when the banks stopped payment in specie. With bank notes now worthless, one bank after another failed.

Too Much Expansion

The earlier years of prosperity had also led to an overexpansion of cotton planting in the South and extensive expansion in manufacturing in the North. Because Great Britain was undergoing its own hard times, there was a sharp decline in the demand for cotton. Work stopped on projects such as highways and canals, and factories were forced to close. Wages for a common laborer in the United States fell to 68 cents for a 14-hour day, and unemployment mounted. Paper money became less valuable and inflation sent food prices spiraling upward. Unable to pay on their bank loans, farmers, plantation owners, and urban business owners were forced to sell their land.

Van Buren had barely taken office when the panic began. A century later, Presidents Herbert Hoover and Franklin D. Roosevelt would feel it was their duty to deal with the Great Depression. In Van Buren's time, however, it is doubtful that any President would have conceived of a depression as other than a problem for the business community to handle. Van Buren felt obligated to put the government on a sound basis, but the ills of unemployment and falling farm prices were left to be tackled by business. As the depression deepened, a disgruntled populace put more and more of the blame for it on the Van Buren administration.

NOMINATION POLITICS

The depression played right into the hands of the Whigs. When the Democrats lost both Houses of Congress in 1838, a Whig victory seemed inevitable, if only the various party factions could hold together during the 1840 campaign.

The obvious Whig candidate for President was Henry Clay. He had been one of the first to fight against Jackson, he had been one of the leaders of the new party, and he had been running for the office since 1824. He had been nominated by the Whigs in 1832 but lost to Jackson and was passed over in 1836. But Clay was confident that 1840 was the year he would win the much-coveted prize.

However, in order to win, Clay needed the support of the southern Whigs. To do that, he began to abandon some of the ideas in his American System, such as the national bank and the protective tariff. Clay's compromise with his principles proved fruitless.

The northern Whigs, such as William Seward, Thaddeus Stevens, and Daniel Webster, were convinced that no slaveowner like Clay could carry the two states needed to win an election—New York and Pennsylvania. The only other possibilities were General William Henry Harrison and Winfield Scott.

The Whig National Convention

At the Whig National Convention in December 1839, James Barbour, the governor of Virginia, was elected permanent chairman and Tyler was honored by being selected as one of 13 convention vice-presidents. The task of selecting the Whig nominees for President and Vice-President was given to a general committee composed of representatives from the state delegations. After the committee had made its selections, the convention as a whole would ratify the committee's choices.

Despite Clay's devious behavior during the contested U.S. Senate race in Virginia between Tyler and Rives, Tyler was convinced that Clay was the best presidential candidate. Of the three possibilities—Clay, Harrison, and Scott—Tyler felt that Clay was the best known, the most intelligent, and the most experienced in politics. Tyler's support, however, was not enough for Clay to realize his dream. At the end of the second day, Harrison, with the support of Thurlow Weed and the New York delegation, was announced as the party's candidate for President. No one seemed more genuinely disappointed than John Tyler.

Winning the Second Prize

Up to this point in the convention, little attention had been paid to the selection of a vice-presidential candidate. Once Harrison's nomination was confirmed, there was general agreement that the Vice-President had to be from the South in order to balance the ticket. John Tyler seemed the logical candidate. With his name on the ballot in the 1836 election, he was already known to Whig voters. He was a strong advocate of states' rights, and his loyalty to Clay had been much admired. Tyler's nomination would be a peace offering to Clay and his followers.

Other names were offered—Daniel Webster of Massachusetts, Benjamin W. Leigh of Virginia, John M. Clayton of Delaware—but none seemed interested in the job. As is often the case with the vice-presidential nomination, it is offered as a reward for years of service to a political party. It was deemed so unimportant that the Whigs never bothered to seek out Tyler's views or to require him to make any pledges. But Tyler did agree to withdraw from the deadlocked Senate race in Virginia. At a Whig dinner in 1840, Tyler could honestly say, "I do declare, in the presence of my Heavenly Judge, that the nomination given to me was neither solicited nor expected."

The Democratic convention was not held until May 1840, and the outcome was as expected. President Van Buren was renominated unanimously. Colonel Richard M. Johnson, the incumbent Vice-President, remained on the ticket. The campaign that ensued was filled with babble, humbug, and deceit, particularly by the Whigs.

"LOG CABIN AND HARD CIDER"

The meaningless slogan, "Tippecanoe and Tyler, Too," which had been used by the Whigs in 1836, was revived. But a story in the Baltimore *Republican*, a Democratic newspaper, gave the Whigs a far more colorful slogan. After Harrison's nomination, the paper's Washington reporter suggested that the Whigs set Harrison aside and put Clay in his place. When someone asked how this could be done, the reporter answered, "that upon the condition of his receiving a pension of two thousand dollars and a barrel of cider, General Harrison would no doubt consent to withdraw his pretensions, and spend the rest of his days in a log cabin on the banks of the Ohio."

The image of Harrison created by that casual remark was exactly what the Whigs were looking for—that of a simple farmer living in a log cabin and drinking hard cider. The new Whig slogan became "Log Cabin and Hard Cider," and at every political rally a log cabin with a cider barrel in front became the party headquarters.

A Phony Image

The image was as phony as a three-dollar bill, but a gullible public seemed to love it. Harrison was descended from an aristocratic Virginia family and lived in Ohio as a country gentleman in a 16-room mansion. But because part of the house was made of logs covered with weatherboarding, it could be argued that he lived in a log cabin. It made little matter to the Whig Party as long as western farmers, living in log cabins, were favorably impressed.

The Whigs also took every opportunity to ridicule Martin Van Buren as an aristocrat who lived in "a palace," (the White House) and banqueted on gourmet food eaten with gold spoons. But in fact, Van Buren was the self-made man; Harrison was the aristocrat.

Little to Say

Many of the voters were illiterate and uncritical. There were few amusements, and political meetings offered the dramatic quality of the theater combined with the charms of a circus and tavern. For the men, it was a day away from the drudgery of the farm. For the women, it was a day away from all the cares and chores of the home. All were easily reached by the emotional appeal. People were more impressed with the colorful displays and enthusiastic demonstrations than with any serious discussions of the issues.

In most political campaigns, a parade and marching bands are just preliminaries to the big event—the speeches by and for the candidates. But in the Whig campaign of 1840, the food, the drink, and the parade were of even far more importance than usual because the Whigs had so little to say. The candidates were loathe to speak on the issues because any topic a Whig candidate might address could easily be challenged by an opposition faction of the party. In the North, for example, Webster pleased audiences by arguing for a Bank of the United States. In the South, Henry A. Wise campaigned against it.

The goal of the speeches of Harrison and Tyler (when he was forced to speak) was to be as noncommittal as possible on any important questions. It was only when Colonel Johnson made a vigorous campaign in the West that Tyler was forced to go out on a speaking campaign in western Virginia, eastern Ohio, and southwestern Pennsylvania. Tyler found it a most distasteful and depressing experience.

Walking a Tightrope

Tyler also found it difficult to avoid the issues, especially when hecklers in the audience demanded answers. Once, speaking at a Whig convention in Pittsburgh, Pennsylvania, he was forced to admit that he approved of Clay's Compromise of 1833, despite the fact that the Whigs in that city had called for repeal of that legislation. It was one of the few times that he gave a thoroughly forthright answer, but he was sure to link it with Whig Party favorites. "I am," he said, "in favor of what General Harrison and Mr. Clay are in favor of; I am in favor of preserving the compromise bill as it now stands; between General Harrison, Mr. Clay, and myself, there is no difference of opinion on this subject."

Tyler really had no alternative. If he was as open and honorable as he prided himself in being, he would have jeopardized the election. Undoubtedly, he felt the vice-presidential candidate had no right to do that to his party. Perhaps he should never have accepted the nomination in a party in which the majority of members advocated measures that he had opposed throughout his political career. In view of the fact that the party had no platform, no set of principles to which he was honor-bound, Tyler did what he had to in order to win the election. Whenever possible, he sidestepped the issues.

A WHIG VICTORY

The mudslinging and the circus atmosphere of the Whig campaign outdid anything that the Democrats had developed in the Jackson years. The American people must have loved it, because when the votes were counted, the Harrison-Tyler ticket won. Hundreds of thousands of new voters had flocked to the polls. The Whigs cut deeply into the vote of the southern rural farmer, who had been pro-Democratic since Jackson's election in 1828. In the West, the voters flocked to the frontier image of Old Tippecanoe, just as they had flocked to Old Hickory only a few years before. And the northern Whigs held strong. Though Harrison received 234 electoral

*President William Henry Harrison served the shortest
presidency in American history. He died just one month after
his inauguration and was succeeded by his Vice-President,
John Tyler. (Library of Congress.)*

votes to 60 for Van Buren, Harrison led by only 150,000 of the 2,400,000 popular votes cast. Tyler was dismayed to learn that Virginia, his and Harrison's home state, had defected to Van Buren. The only consolation was that Van Buren lost New York, his native state.

Harrison had already publicly admitted that he would serve only one term (leaving the door open to Clay in 1844). Harrison also leaned strongly to the idea that the authority to lead the country lay not in the presidency, but in the Congress and the Cabinet. Such ideas had led Whig leaders to believe that in the Harrison administration, Clay would be "the man behind the throne." They—and Tyler—would soon find these beliefs well-founded.

The Shortest Term in History

There were several Whigs who, during the course of the campaign, voiced concern about the 68-year-old general's health. But none could have predicted that the Harrison administration would be the shortest in American history.

It was a cold, rainy March day in 1841 when Harrison, mounted on a prancing white horse and obviously enjoying the cheers of the Washington crowd, rode to his inauguration. At noon, the Senate convened and the oath of office was administered to John Tyler. With "much grace, dignity, and self-possession," he delivered a brief five-minute address. Then Harrison was escorted to the eastern portico (porch) of the Capitol. There the oath of office was administered and the new President gave a two-hour inaugural address. The new administration had officially begun.

John Tyler returned to Williamsburg. He expected that he would return to Washington as chairman of the Senate when it convened and that he would participate in social occasions connected with his position. Beyond that, he looked forward

In this wood engraving done in 1888, Vice-President John Tyler is shown receiving the news of President Harrison's death. On the morning of April 5, 1841, two messengers dismounted at the gate of Tyler's home in Williamsburg and awakened the Vice-President with the startling news that President Harrison had died the day before. One of the men was Daniel Webster's son. By 4:00 A.M. the next morning, Tyler had made the 230-mile journey to Washington and prepared to take over the reins of government. (Library of Congress.)

to four years of relative peace and quiet in the comforts of his home. Tyler's dream was short-lived.

A Sick President

The responsibilities quickly began to take their toll on the new President. In addition, he had caught a cold during his inaugural address, and it quickly worsened. The daily flood of office-seekers taxed the President's endurance, and the arrival of Henry Clay did not help. Clay began to press for his own demands. One was for calling an early session of Congress. The second was for the appointment of John M. Clayton to the Cabinet position of secretary of the treasury. Harrison finally lost his temper and shouted, "Mr. Clay, you forget that *I* am President!"

The pressures sapped Harrison's strength. On March 24, his cold turned into severe pneumonia and on April 4, at 12:30 A.M., only one month after his inauguration, Harrison died.

On April 5, John Tyler was awakened by the sound of impatient knocking at his door. Two somber-faced men had arrived from Washington, Daniel Webster's son, chief clerk of the State Department, and a Mr. Beall, an officer of the Senate. They had been sent by the Cabinet to notify the Vice-President that President Harrison had died.

With remarkable speed for those days, Tyler made the journey of 230 miles, arriving in the nation's capital at four o'clock in the morning of April 6. Vice-President John Tyler was about to take charge.

Chapter 7

The Accidental President

John Tyler had one of the stormiest administrations of any American President. He assumed office without the backing of a political party, and he battled an opposition in Congress led by a strong and charismatic leader, Henry Clay, once a dear friend.

At 51 years of age, Tyler was, at that time, the youngest President to take office. He was also the first to succeed to the position following the unexpected death of the President. As an ardent supporter of the Constitution, Tyler must have recognized that what he did, as he moved from the vice-presidency to the presidency, would set a precedent for the future. The question was: Should the former Vice-President assume all the power, duties, and dignity of a regular President or should he be regarded merely as one who is taking care of the daily duties of administration until the next election? Does he merely *act* as President or does he vacate the vice-presidency to *become* the President?

INTERPRETING THE CONSTITUTION

The Constitution states: "In case of the removal of the President from office, or of his death, resignation or inability to discharge the powers and duties of the said office, *the same* shall devolve [be handed down] on the Vice-President." It is not clear whether "the same" refers to the duties or the office.

Tyler, a strict constructionist of the Constitution, decided this time to choose a broad interpretation. He claimed all the rights and privileges of the presidency, a precedent followed by future Vice-Presidents who became chief executive under similar circumstances. He made this interpretation secure by insisting on taking the oath of President, moving into the White House, and making an inaugural address. Tyler was now a President in his own right and not merely a caretaker of the dead President's administration.

A Low Opinion

Tyler's decision stirred much debate in the newspapers, and it was not easily swallowed by all of the Whig and Democratic leaders. Among those Whigs who insisted that Tyler was only an *acting* President was former President John Quincy Adams, whose opinion of Tyler was rather poor. On the day that Harrison died, Adams included this passage in his diary: "Tyler is a political sectarian [narrow-minded person] of the slave-driving, Virginian, Jeffersonian school, principled against all improvement, with all the interests and passions and vices of slavery rooted in his moral and political constitution — with talents not above mediocrity [of moderate or low value]. . . . No one ever thought of his being placed in the executive chair."

When Congress met in a special session on May 31, 1841, the legality of Tyler's position was again challenged. Senator William Allen of Ohio suggested that the Senate, in its communication with John Tyler, address him as "the Vice-President, on whom, by the death of the late President, the powers and duties of President have devolved." That measure was voted down by a vote of 38 to 8. The issue, however, would plague Tyler even after he left the White House. In 1848 Tyler was forced to return a package to Senator James Buchanan, later President of the United States, because he persisted in addressing Tyler as "ex-vice-president."

A Sore Loser

Clay had not been a gracious loser when he lost the Whig Party's nomination to Harrison in 1840. When Harrison had openly stated that he would serve for only one term, Clay had set his sights on the presidency in 1844. Now, with Tyler as President, the nomination did not seem quite as certain. If Tyler turned out to be a successful President, the Whig nomination might not be offered to the senator from Kentucky in 1844.

Clay was not modest about his talents or his power. He was the recognized leader of the nationalist Whigs, the majority Whig faction, a group unwilling to accept the new President with his states' rights view. Clay assumed that President Tyler, a courtly southern gentleman with mild manners, would be as easy to control as President Harrison. But Clay would soon discover that beneath John Tyler's soft-mannered exterior was a man with a strong backbone and a mind of his own.

The Cabinet Convenes

Tyler's next problem was how to deal with Harrison's Cabinet. With the exception of Secretary of State Daniel Webster and Postmaster General Francis Granger, the rest of the Cabinet members were in the Clay camp. Tyler knew that he could not expect full cooperation from these Clay admirers. To ask for their resignations would result in a serious break within

In 1850, Henry Clay, though in failing health, argued for the passage of his bill, the Compromise of 1850. His passionate appeal to both the North and the South helped to win support for the measure and delayed the Civil War for another 10 years. (Library of Congress.)

the Whig Party. He had little choice but to proceed with Harrison's appointees.

Tyler did, however, gather a small group of loyal friends who shared his views on states' rights. These men became his personal advisors. Among them were Representative Henry A. Wise and Senator Rives. Tyler's enemies derisively labeled these men Tyler's "kitchen Cabinet." To the President, they proved to be ardent supporters and wise counselors.

What to Expect

At the very first Cabinet meeting, Tyler quickly put his stamp on the type of relationship he expected between the Cabinet members and himself by declaring his independence from Harrison's manner of operation. When Webster explained that Harrison determined policy decisions by a majority vote of the Cabinet members, Tyler bluntly but politely informed the men otherwise. "I shall be pleased to avail myself of your counsel and advice. But I can never consent to being dictated to as to what I shall or shall not do. . . . When you think otherwise, your resignations will be accepted." Though this statement must have made the men uneasy, not one of them resigned.

Tyler's inaugural address, delivered three days after taking office, must have alerted the nationalist Whigs as to what they might expect from his administration. Whereas Harrison had condemned Jackson's use of the veto power, Tyler inferred that he might have to veto measures that were not in keeping with his principles. Harrison had spoken strongly against the increase of presidential power; Tyler said nothing on the issue. Harrison had announced that he would not serve a second term; Tyler was silent on the subject. Those who listened carefully to what was said—or unsaid—could sense that Tyler was not going to be a Harrison clone. He was going to be his own man.

CLAY VERSUS TYLER

Shortly after taking office, President Harrison, at Clay's urging, agreed to call the first session of Congress on May 31, 1841. Tyler now decided to use this first meeting with Congress to explore some ideas, hoping to win some converts to his side. As the session opened, Senator Clay of Kentucky was arrogantly confident. He was not only Senate majority leader, he was head of the party, and he acted as if he were a prime minister.

Tyler began with a gesture designed to reconcile differences. He suggested that Congress repay the Harrison family for the many expenses it had incurred in its move to and from Washington. He also spoke briefly about the need for a firm hand in dealing with foreign policy. He did not sidestep the subject of the nation's finances, but suggested that a new agency be found to handle government revenues. He reminded the members that should any such agency be in conflict with the Constitution, he would reserve the right to reject it.

Clay was determined that the agency was going to be another Bank of the United States. It was also going to be the issue over which he would wrest control from the President. Many historians believe that what eventually became a government crisis was an act that Clay deliberately created for his own political purposes. Whether this was so or not, Clay used Tyler's first congressional session to once more press for his "American System," which included the national bank, a protective tariff, and internal improvements—all issues which Tyler opposed.

Battle Lines Drawn

A month before the opening of the first session of Congress, Tyler wrote to Clay and asked him not to introduce the bank problem or other complex questions until he had time to form a plan of action. Clay chose to ignore Tyler's wishes. Once the bank issue was opened, Tyler attempted to grab the initiative. He offered Clay a plan that would avoid the constitutional objections of the states' rights group.

The plan Tyler proposed had been enthusiastically endorsed by Webster and only reluctantly accepted by the other Cabinet members. Clay flatly rejected it. The long friendship between the two men seemed at an end. Without mincing any words, the President made clear what their future relations would be. In a firm voice, Tyler announced, "Go you now, then, Mr. Clay, to your end of the avenue, where stands the Capitol, and there perform your duty to the country as you shall think proper. So help me God, I shall do mine at this end of it as I think proper." The battle lines were now drawn.

Choosing Weapons

What weapons did each of the contestants have? Besides his skills as a charismatic legislative leader, Clay represented the dominant wing of the Whig Party and held the party whip. He could force party members to follow his direction by denying them good committee assignments or by denying them help with pet bills.

The President had such a small following in Congress that the group was jokingly called "the Corporal's Guard." Nor could he count on support against Clay from his own Cabinet members. One weapon that he might have used was patronage, the privilege of appointing people to office. But a Clay-controlled Senate could hold up or refuse to accept such appointments.

There was one other weapon that the President could use — the veto, the power to refuse to sign legislation passed by Congress. Up until the time of Andrew Jackson, few Presidents had dared to use it, for it invariably aroused angry feelings in Congress. Jackson had used the veto effectively because his overwhelming popularity in his elections had proven that the people were behind him. Tyler could not claim any such support. He had been swept into office by the enthusiasm for Harrison and a quirk of fate.

The opponents were hardly evenly matched. Tyler was left with either swallowing all the nationalist principles of his opponent and becoming a decorative but ineffective President, or he could stand firm for what he believed in, be left with his self-respect, and face four years of dissension. He chose the latter course.

THE BANK ISSUE—AGAIN

The bank plan that Clay presented to Congress was much like the old national bank. The bank would also have the power to establish branches where and when it wished. Since the new bank plan did not require the consent of the states, it was a red flag for those who supported states' rights. Clay soon realized that he would need a few more votes to pass his plan.

Tyler, too, was working on a plan with Secretary of the Treasury Thomas Ewing, and early in June, it was ready. The plan provided a central bank in Washington, D.C., with branches located in several states *with their consent.* Had Clay endorsed Ewing's plan, it probably would have been adopted by Congress without much change. Tyler would have signed it and a fight between Tyler and the Whig majority might have been avoided. Clay, however, chose to reject Ewing's plan.

Presidential Choice—a Veto

The twists of fate and politics are often difficult to explain. Two of the members of Congress who offered alternative bank plans were from Tyler's home state. One was Senator William Rives, once Tyler's foe in the contested Senate race. He was now a staunch champion of the President. The other was Representative John Minor Botts, who had sided with Tyler *against* the election of Rives. He was now Clay's loyal lieutenant.

Late in July, Clay accepted a bill that included the Botts proposal. The bill that was offered satisfied none of the factions. Nevertheless, it was passed by a bare majority: 25–24 in the Senate and 26–23 in the House. It was rushed through the House of Representatives with only four days' discussion on what was undoubtedly the most important bill of the session.

In the Cabinet, the bank bill was discussed at length. All the members recommended that the President sign it. During the 10-day waiting period before a President has to decide whether to accept or reject a bill, Tyler gave no hint as to what his intentions were. The bank bill was hotly debated by members in the halls of Congress, by coachmen in the streets, and by bank executives over lunch. Would the President sign it or not? There were even those who were willing to make bets on the presidential decision.

The opinion that the President might veto the bill was strengthened when his son, Robert, in discussing the subject with a representative in the lobby of the House said, "To suppose that [my] father could be gulled by such a humbug compromise as the bill contained, was to suppose he was an ass."

The President waited until the tenth day and then sent a message with his secretary, John Tyler, Jr., to the Senate.

The White House during Tyler's administration. Shortly after Tyler assumed his duties as President, serious conflicts arose between him and the Whigs. He soon became a President without a party. Among other difficulties, he suffered a shortage of funds needed for repairs at the presidential mansion. Yet, he was always a gracious host and when Julia Gardiner became his second wife, he was better able to entertain in a manner befitting a President. (Library of Congress.)

All other business was stopped immediately. Silence reigned as the message was read. The President's decision—with supporting reasons for his action—was a veto.

Appalling Conduct

There was a spattering of applause, given by striking the floor with canes. But there were also a few hisses. Several of the senators were appalled at such conduct, and Senator Thomas Benton declared that such behavior was an insult to the President and to the Senate. He made a motion that the offenders be arrested. Senator Rives and Senator James Buchanan, who later became President himself, tried to stop the motion, arguing that Tyler would never deny a citizen the right of free speech or expression. When the culprit admitted his error and apologized, the motion was withdrawn.

The President's spirits were lifted when a group of Democratic Senators visited the White House to congratulate Tyler on "his patriotic courage and courageous action." But Tyler was dismayed when, after midnight, a mob of about 30 people appeared under the White House windows, blowing trumpets and shouting "Huzza for Clay!" and "Down with the veto!" He was especially perturbed because Mrs. Tyler, who had been paralyzed by a stroke two years earlier, was awakened and terrified by the terrible noise outside.

When the ruffians who had participated in the midnight disturbance were apprehended and brought to trial, Tyler wrote a letter to the prosecuting attorney. The President asked that the culprits not be prosecuted further on the grounds that the demonstration "was one of those outbreaks of popular feeling incident, in some degree, to our form of government, and entirely evanescent [apt to disappear] and harmless in character."

VETOES AND RESIGNATIONS

Two days after Tyler's veto of the bank bill, Clay arose in the Senate and demanded that the President bow to the will of the people or resign. In view of the one-vote margin by which the bill passed in the Senate, the measure was hardly the "will of the people." Yet Clay persisted and called for a motion to override the veto. But the 25–24 vote was not enough to meet the two-thirds vote needed to set aside a presidential veto.

Realizing that the bill could not be passed over Tyler's veto, Whig leaders sent two emissaries to the President to find out what kind of legislation he would accept. Tyler gave them some general ideas and assigned two Cabinet members, Secretary of the Treasury Thomas Ewing and Secretary of State Daniel Webster, to meet with the Whig representatives.

When the new bill was offered, Tyler found parts of it still unacceptable. He then notified members of the House of Representatives that the bill did not have his full approval unless certain changes were made. Nevertheless, the final document, without any changes, was rushed through both Houses of Congress. Once again, the President vetoed it.

The Cabinet Resigns

Two days after the second veto and a meeting with Clay, all of the members of the Cabinet except Daniel Webster resigned. When Webster revealed his decision to stay on, the President rose and offered his hand. "Give me your hand on that," he said warmly, "and now I will say to you that Henry Clay is a doomed man."

Why did Webster choose to stay on with an administration that was faltering? For one thing, he thoroughly enjoyed his honored role as secretary of state, and he was in the midst

*Though he lusted after the presidency for himself, Daniel
Webster proved to be a good friend to John Tyler. Webster
served as a loyal and valuable secretary of state during most
of Tyler's administration.* (Library of Congress.)

of important negotiations with the British minister. He hoped that a satisfactory agreement with Great Britain would add to his personal prestige and encourage thoughts of his being Tyler's successor. Moreover, if he resigned his Cabinet seat, it would appear to ally him with Clay and put him under Clay's authority. Webster was too much his own man to put himself in that position.

The President was better prepared for the resignations of his Cabinet than his enemies expected. And he was not particularly unhappy at the prospect of being able to put his own choices in the Cabinet rather than Harrison's or Clay's. With the aid of his "kitchen Cabinet," (his personal advisors), Tyler quickly chose the new Cabinet members and submitted their names to the Senate before it could adjourn. The Senate could find no reason to reject the nominees, and they were confirmed. Clay had not succeeded in isolating the President.

But the matter was far from closed. The second veto of the bank bill had aroused the Whig members of Congress as they had never been aroused before. To the Whigs, Tyler's second veto was the ultimate act of defiance. On September 13, 1841, the day that Congress adjourned, 50 dedicated Whig members of Congress met on Capitol Square. They announced that the alliance between the President and the Whigs was at an end. Tyler was now a President without a party!

Chapter **8**

A President Without a Party

In cities all over the country Tyler's burning effigy lighted up the darkness of the streets. In the White House, he received hundreds of letters containing threats of assassination. It was a heartbreaking time. The President sorely needed the warmth and loyalty of family and friends.

From his family, Tyler received his greatest comfort and support. Robert Tyler became the President's chief liaison to the Conservative Democrats in Philadelphia and New York City, and John Tyler, Jr., wrote pamphlets and publicized the President's views on a series of issues. His lovely daughter-in-law, Priscilla, worked hard to keep the bad news from Letitia, whose physical condition continued to worsen.

Tyler's friends in the "kitchen Cabinet" were supportive, and the besieged President deeply appreciated the loyalty of Secretary of State Daniel Webster, whose national reputation also gave Tyler a political base in the North.

A CABINET TO HIS LIKING

Tyler would make more than 19 appointments to fill the five Cabinet posts. Three men died in office and two were not confirmed by the Senate. The other vacancies were due to resignations.

Some of these resignations were probably due to Tyler's desire to appoint men who were competent—but who would follow his policies with a minimum of opposition. Tyler rejected the belief held by Clay and other Whigs that, in Cabinet councils, the President is merely one among equals. Though willing to listen to the ideas and criticisms of his Cabinet members, he held firm to the idea that the President alone is responsible for executive decisions. When the decision was made, he expected support without reservation from his Cabinet. As time went on, the Tyler Cabinet increasingly was dominated by a states' rights group with Democratic leanings.

Into the Shadows

Even before the mass exit of the Tyler Cabinet, John Calhoun predicted that the defeat of the bank bill by presidential veto "would probably break up the Whig Party and lead to a remodeling of the Cabinet." By September 1841, Calhoun's prediction had been partially realized, for the Cabinet was remodeled according to Tyler's wishes. And by the time of the next midterm congressional election in 1842, the Whig Party was beginning to lose its power. The Whig majority of 60 in the House of Representatives gave way to a Democratic majority of 80.

The Whig Party would have one more chance for the presidency, but the prize would not be won by the perennial candidate, Henry Clay. In 1848, the man who became President was a stocky, former general, the most politically inexperienced man elected to the presidency up to that time—"Old Rough and Ready" Zachary Taylor. When Taylor died in office after serving only 16 months, he was succeeded by the ineffective Millard Fillmore. By the 1850s, the Whig Party was in total disarray, and a new party would begin to take its place.

PROBLEMS AND MORE PROBLEMS

The national bank was now a dead issue. Tyler had vetoed the bill that Clay and the Congress had offered, and they, in turn, had rejected a compromise, the Exchequer Plan, which the President had devised and which had been praised and approved by the Cabinet. Now, the problem that desperately needed the attention and efforts of both the executive and legislative branches of the government was the economy. When Congress assembled for its regular session in December 1841, the two controversial items to be dealt with were—once again—the tariff and the proposal to distribute to the states the monies received from the sale of federal lands.

Different Viewpoints

The budget report clearly spelled out the urgency of the problem. There would be a deficit of 14 million dollars unless immediate measures were taken to increase revenues. In an era when the income tax did not exist, the obvious answer was to increase the tariff rate. Both Congress and the President disliked raising the rate above the 20 percent agreed upon in the Compromise Tariff of 1833. However, both were willing to face the challenge of amending the bill—but for totally different reasons.

Tyler favored a tariff increase as the best means of obtaining revenue to run the government. Clay and the protectionists saw the increase primarily as a favor to American manufacturers. The same group also favored the distribution of revenues from public land sales to the states. The generosity of this move would reap political benefits and be much appreciated by states struggling to survive the depression.

Two Vetoes

Tyler saw the distribution of land funds quite differently. Twice during the summer of 1842, Congress passed bills that called for higher tariffs *and* distribution of land revenues to the states. Twice Tyler was compelled to veto the measures. In a message to Congress, Tyler explained his reasons:

> The Treasury is in a state of extreme embarrassment, requiring every dollar which it can make available, and when the government had not only to lay additional taxes, but to borrow money . . . the bill proposes to give away a fruitful source of revenue [the monies from the sale of public land]. . . . I must regard [this] as highly impolitic.

Following his second veto, the attacks on Tyler became more violent than ever. The *Daily Richmond Whig* declared, "Again has the imbecile, into whose hands accident has placed the power, vetoed a bill passed by the majority of those legally authorized to pass it."

Impeachment Considered

A House committee was organized to investigate the reasons for Tyler's vetoes. It was headed by John Quincy Adams, no admirer of Tyler, and weighted heavily with other anti-Tylerites. The result was as expected – a free-swinging attack on Tyler's administration. The report recommended an amendment to the Constitution that would allow Congress to override a presidential veto by a simple majority vote. It concluded by stating that John Tyler was a fit subject for impeachment proceedings. A minority report was issued, but it was signed by only two Democratic congressmen, Charles J. Ingersoll of Pennsylvania and James I. Roosevelt of New York.

In July, John M. Botts, another enemy of Tyler's, called for a committee to investigate the President's conduct in office with a view toward impeachment. The impeachment proceedings were finally squashed in January 1843, with a vote of 127 to 83 against the idea. By that time, the midterm congressional election of 1842 had already vindicated Tyler. The people might not be behind him; but they had certainly begun to reject the Whigs.

The "Black" Tariff

While the impeachment debate was still going on, Tyler realized that government operations would grind to a halt unless funds could be found to meet expenses. His first priority had to be a revenue bill. Accordingly, on August 30, 1842, Tyler at last signed a bill that had been pushed by Democrats and protectionist Whigs. Although the Tariff Act of 1842, called the "Black Tariff" by southern antiprotectionists, raised rates higher than the President would have wished, Tyler never publicly gave his reasons for accepting the measure. There is no doubt he was fearful that the federal government would be forced into bankruptcy if immediate action was not taken. His approval of the act was also partly due to the fact that the bill made no mention of the distribution of land revenues to the states. And he was emotionally drained from the Whig assaults and the talk of impeachment. Letitia was dying and he was deeply concerned that her peace of mind not be disturbed during her last days.

SAD DAYS AND HAPPY MOMENTS

Though it had been expected, Letitia's death on September 10, 1842, left the close-knit family with a great sense of loss. All during her long illness, Tyler had protected her from the anger and hostility that surrounded his administration. Only once had she even been able to leave her sickroom to attend a White House function, and that was for the wedding of her daughter, Elizabeth. It was an intimate family affair.

When Letitia died, the newspapers ceased their hostile

statements against her husband long enough to pay tribute to her virtues as a wife and mother. The funeral was held in the White House, and then Mrs. Tyler was laid to rest in New Kent County, Virginia, near her childhood home.

Letitia's death affected the entire family. Priscilla agonized, "Nothing can exceed the loneliness of this large and gloomy mansion, hung with black, its walls echoing with sighs." As a form of therapy, the President busied himself with his work and corresponding with his children. The letters served to bring him closer to his daughters, particularly after Letitia's death.

Tyler also found a diversion from his grief by purchasing a piece of property close to Greenway, his boyhood home. It is said he renamed the property Sherwood Forest in a humorous reference to his outlaw status in the Whig Party. Though it was an expensive undertaking, probably one he could ill-afford, Tyler spent many hours remodeling the estate, sketching and planning additional rooms, and working on such details as how the chimney should be built and how the stairways should be pitched.

White House Hostess

During his wife's illness, Tyler had kept this depressing aspect of his life strictly private. Yet during his tenure as President, the White House was a place of warmth and social hospitality. Much of the credit for this can be attributed to the personality of the President's daughter-in-law, Priscilla Tyler. Because Tyler's two older daughters were married and busy with their families in Virginia, and the two younger ones were not old enough to take on the responsibility, it fell to Priscilla to perform the task of White House hostess, normally the function of the First Lady.

The lovely Priscilla was perfect for the role. She treated the White House as a stage and performed her duties with elegance, charm, and good humor. She was also wise enough to seek the advice of Dolley Madison, the great hostess during the Jefferson and Madison administrations. Priscilla supervised and presided over two formal dinner parties a week, occasional small private balls, and a grand reception once a month when Congress was in session. Sometimes, more than 1,000 people attended these events, making it almost impossible to dance or to even move about.

An Embarrassing Incident

Only once did Priscilla fail to live up to Tyler's description of her as the "presiding genius of the White House." The incident occurred on the night of the first formal dinner for the members of the Cabinet. Priscilla, already pregnant with her second child, had had an exhausting day with her fretful four-month old daughter and with making plans for the dinner. By the time evening came, she was overtired and tense. Seated next to Secretary of State Daniel Webster, she blithely carried on a conversation, not a bit awed by Webster's booming voice or imposing manner.

But as dessert was being passed, Priscilla suddenly turned white and then fell from the table in a faint. Gallantly, Webster swooped her up in his arms to carry her away from the table when her husband rushed over with a pitcher of ice water. In the confusion that ensued, Robert Tyler dumped the ice water over both Priscilla's new dress and the secretary of state. As Priscilla later described the incident in a letter, the water ruined her "lovely new dress, and I am afraid, produced a decided coolness between myself and the secretary of state. I had to be taken to my room, and poor Mr. Webster had to be shaken off, dried and brushed, before he could resume dinner."

The incident did not mar their relationship, for Webster became one of Priscilla's favorite Washington figures and he, in turn, became her advisor on the subject of foods and wines.

A MASTER OF DIPLOMACY

If ever there was a place where John Tyler's natural courtesy, charm, and tact could win friends, it was in the arena of foreign relations. His ability to make others feel at ease oiled the wheels of international negotiations, preventing the kind of friction that often occurs in tense situations. This was particularly true in his government's relations with Great Britain.

When Tyler came to the presidency, there were three disputes which threatened relations between the United States and Great Britain. The first problem, the *Caroline* incident and its aftermath, the McLeod Case, he inherited from the Van Buren administration.

In 1837 a group of Canadians revolted against British authority, winning the sympathy of some American citizens along the Canadian border. An American ship, the *Caroline*, proceeded to give aid to the rebels. While it was on the American side of the Niagara River, the *Caroline* was set on fire by a Canadian expedition and allowed to drift over Niagara Falls. During the attack, an American citizen named Durfree was killed.

State Versus Federal Jurisdiction

The anger over the affair had pretty much died down when, three years later, a Canadian citizen, Alexander McLeod, boasted while drunk that it was he who had killed Durfree in the *Caroline* incident. Since the event took place on the American side of the border, McLeod was promptly arrested by New York authorities and charged with murder and arson. The British strongly protested, arguing that McLeod had been acting under British military orders during a wartime situation and, therefore, he could not be prosecuted. Great Britain "formally demanded" that McLeod be released, threatening serious consequences if this were not done.

However, under the American judicial system at the time,

New York State had complete jurisdiction over a case of murder. The President was powerless. All that Washington could do was to bring pressure on the state to transfer the case to a federal court. With passions so high along the border states, New York was not about to meet that request.

McLeod was brought to trial in Utica, New York, where the town teemed with strangers and talk of lynching filled the air. Tyler sent his attorney general to Utica to ensure that the trial was fairly carried out. Fortunately for all concerned, the case for the prosecution was weak. McLeod was able to convince a not-very-sympathetic jury that he had been five or six miles away at the time of the *Caroline* raid and, after only 20 minutes of deliberation, the jury acquitted him of the murder charge.

Tyler, an experienced lawyer, was greatly relieved by the outcome. Here was a case where one state could have provoked a war that all the other states would have had to fight. To prevent such a possibility in the future, Daniel Webster, with Tyler's approval, drafted a bill that Congress passed in August 1842. Under this act, the federal courts, rather than state courts, were given the right to prosecute cases in which aliens were charged with crimes committed while under the authority of a foreign government.

The Webster–Ashburton Treaty

The most important point of friction between England and the United States was one that was as old as the nation itself. This was the dispute over the boundary between the state of Maine and New Brunswick, a province in Canada. In 1838–1839, clashes along the border threatened the peace, and attempts to negotiate a settlement seemed futile. It was one of the most pressing problems left to Tyler by President Van Buren.

It was most fortunate that the British selected a man eminently qualified and particularly acceptable to the United

States to negotiate the border problem and other matters. Alexander Baring, first Lord Ashburton, had been a member of Parliament, his wife was the daughter of a prominent American, and he had worked hard to promote peace and friendship between England and the United States.

After Lord Ashburton arrived in Washington in April 1842, he and the members of his party went out of their way to initiate negotiations in a friendly fashion. Public officials and socialites returned his gracious efforts with a round of parties in his honor. The President himself, with Priscilla acting as hostess, made such an elegant affair to honor Lord Ashburton that even the normally negative John Quincy Adams admitted, "The courtesies of the President and Mrs. R. Tyler to their guests were all that the most accomplished European court could have displayed."

The Rude Commissioners

Secretary of State Daniel Webster deliberately chose an informal procedure for negotiations between Lord Ashburton and himself. Letters of agreement would not be written until all details had been worked out. The written documents would then be submitted to the President for his approval before being sent to the Senate.

At one point, however, negotiations almost collapsed. The commissioners from Maine were becoming so stubborn and tactless in their responses to Lord Ashburton's requests that, combined with the heat of Washington, he was on the verge of returning home. Webster's nerves, too, were on edge from poor health and the heat, and it was often hard for him to maintain the courtesies needed in diplomacy.

At this point, Tyler recognized the urgency of the situation. He asked to meet with Lord Ashburton. Employing his superb skills as a conversationalist and his customary tact and suave manners, Tyler succeeded in persuading the Englishman to return to the negotiation table.

At the close of negotiations concerning the border issue, the United States received 7,000 of the disputed 12,000 square miles of land, allowing Great Britain to build a much-wanted military road along the 5,000 square miles ceded to it. To sweeten the settlement for Maine and Massachusetts, the federal government gave each state $125 million as compensation for the lands each had to give up. A concession along Lake Superior unwittingly left the United States with the priceless Mesabi Range iron deposits, which were discovered 24 years later.

Slave Ships and Search Parties

The hardest part of the negotiations between the United States and Great Britain dealt with the right of searching slave ships. England had abolished slavery in her overseas colonies and was now taking steps to erase the African slave trade altogether. A nation at war has the right to search neutral ships on the high seas to check for smuggled goods. This is not the case during peacetime, however, unless such a concession is granted by the country whose ship is involved.

Several nations had made such an agreement with Great Britain, permitting the search of their ships for suspected slave cargoes. Since slavery had not yet been abolished in America, the United States refused to grant England any such privilege. Thus, the American flag flew over many a wretched slave vessel. Even without the slavery issue, many U.S. citizens still remembered that the War of 1812 had been fought over such searches of American vessels on the high seas by the British, who captured American seamen and pressed them into service in the British Navy. That memory alone was enough reason not to give the search privilege to Great Britain.

Unlike the border dispute, Ashburton's demands could not be met in this case. Though Tyler continued to affirm his hatred of the slave trade, in his first annual message to Congress, he denied the right of any nation to peacetime searches of American ships on the high seas. However, a compromise gave both nations the right to maintain a naval force off the coast of Africa to enforce the laws dealing with the suppression of the slave trade.

The border issue and that of the slave trade, as well as other less important matters, were put together in one package and offered to the Senate as the Webster–Ashburton Treaty. On August 9, 1842, the treaty was signed; it was ratified by the Senate shortly thereafter by a vote of 29–9 without any changes.

An Insult to the President

Though never fully credited for his role in the Webster–Ashburton Treaty negotiations, Tyler could, nevertheless, take personal satisfaction in the results. A number of critical issues that could have erupted into open hostilities were either settled or swept under the rug. The air had been cleared between the two great English-speaking nations, and each could get on with other business.

The Whigs, however, were not inclined to give the President any credit for his efforts on the treaty. At a dinner in honor of Lord Ashburton in New York the month following the signing of the treaty, a toast was offered to the Queen of England to much applause. A similar toast tendered to President Tyler was greeted with stony silence. When word of this insult leaked out to the people of New York, a large protest meeting was organized and thousands of people marched carrying banners reading "AN INSULT TO THE PRESIDENT IS AN INSULT TO THE NATION." The people of Philadelphia also passed a resolution calling to shame those persons who had participated in the unfortunate affair.

Tyler's efforts in securing peace with Great Britain was one of the great accomplishments of his administration. There would be other accomplishments that would also be successful because of the President's patience, determination, and tact.

Chapter 9

Rebellion and Romance

John Tyler was a "people person." His elegant appearance, charming manners, and magnetic personality served him well whenever he met people. It is sometimes difficult to realize that until the invention of photography in the 1850s, a President's face might never be seen by most of the people unless they saw a painting of him or a caricature in a political cartoon. In fact, in Tyler's time, the bulk of the American people lived and died without ever seeing what a President looked like.

With such personal assets, Tyler might have succeeded in improving his public image and stature had he traveled extensively throughout the nation while he was President. His personal charisma would have done much to undo the terrible picture of him painted in Whig newspapers.

Only once during his administration did Tyler take a journey to another part of the country. That was to Boston in June 1843 to attend a celebration on the completion of the Bunker Hill Monument. En route he visited Wilmington, Delaware; Philadelphia; New York City; and Providence, Rhode Island. Though he had also planned to visit Albany and Buffalo, New York, as well as Cleveland and Cincinnati, Ohio, the death of Attorney General Legare cut short the trip and brought about a hasty return to Washington.

INDIAN WAR AND INSURRECTION

With a hostile press and the Whig Party arrayed against him, Tyler could do little to carry out any measures that required the cooperation of Congress. But when he could act on his own, using his executive powers, Tyler demonstrated strength and an ability for wise action. Two instances where such initiative achieved results were the Seminole War and the Dorr Rebellion.

End of the Seminole War

In 1837 President Jackson decided to move all the Seminole Indians in Florida to an area west of the Mississippi River. Once the tribe had numbered several thousand, most of whom moved to Oklahoma, where about 3,000 descendants live today. By 1842 there were still about 240 Seminoles left in Florida, of whom only about 80 were males of fighting age. Those who were left in Florida were unreachable either for capture or for peace negotiations because they had hidden themselves in the swamps. Recognizing the futility of spending more time and money to chase them down, Tyler simply declared the Seminole War at an end in 1842.

The Dorr Rebellion

While the Webster–Ashburton Treaty negotiations were under way in the spring of 1842, a long-simmering problem in Rhode Island came to a boil. The state had been operating under its outmoded colonial charter of 1663. Without a new state constitution, much of the population was disenfranchised (unable to vote) because one of the voting qualifications was the ownership of fairly high-priced property.

The clamor for a new state constitution became so great that in 1841 an unauthorized convention was called in Rhode Island and a new constitution, called the "People's Constitution," was drawn up. A new state government was created, with Thomas W. Dorr as governor. But Governor King of the charter government saw these activities as an insurrection and called out the state militia to quell any attempts by Dorr's followers to assume power.

Tyler was well aware of the situation in Rhode Island from confidential reports by government agents and because both King and Dorr had made requests for federal aid. The President was in a quandary, however. How could he deny that the people of Rhode Island had a legitimate right to seek the voting privilege for more of its citizens? On the other hand, if Governor King needed federal intervention to maintain law and order, then troops would have to be sent.

President Tyler handled the issue firmly and with caution. He told Governor King that he would send troops *not* to prevent but to put down an insurgency, and *only* if there was an act of violence. He also made it clear to King that a convention should be called to make a more liberal state constitution, and he urged King to offer pardons to the rebels if they promised to support the present government. Tyler also advised Dorr and his followers to seek a course of verbal persuasion in place of violence in order to ensure more "lasting blessings than those accomplished by violence and bloodshed."

Praise at Last

When both sides seemed determined to get their way by using force, Tyler sent the secretary of war to Rhode Island with instructions to use federal troops, if necessary. But when the rebel troops were attacked by the state militia, they fled. Tyler's words had not fallen on deaf ears, for King had not only called a convention, he also made sweeping concessions which greatly increased the number of eligible voters in the state.

As usual, Tyler was criticized for his policy, and his opponents in the House passed a resolution demanding that the

President submit all the documents covering the action of the federal government in the Rhode Island uprising. This time, the President obliged by sending the documents and an explanation of his actions. The evidence overwhelmingly demonstrated that Tyler had conducted the Dorr Rebellion so wisely that even the *National Intelligencer*, a Whig newspaper, lauded the President for his handling of the affair.

ENTER JULIA GARDINER

For some time after Letitia's death, the White House was officially in mourning and social activities were curtailed. Priscilla Tyler tried hard to keep up the family's spirits by occasionally inviting friends in for a quiet evening. Among the personal friends invited to the presidential mansion in December following Letitia's death were members of the Gardiner family. David Gardiner was a New York state senator, and his visit to Washington with his charming family during the winter of 1841–1842 had made quite a splash on the social scene. Now the family had returned for the winter social season of 1842–1843.

The first Gardiner arrived in America in the early 1600s, and over the years the family had become well respected and wealthy. David Gardiner's two daughters, Julia and Margaret, both beautiful and bright, had created quite a stir among the young and not-so-young bachelors when they were last in the nation's capital. The Tyler sons, married or not, were also taken with the charm of these young women. And Juliana, the aristocratic mother of the Gardiner family, was equally taken with the courtesies and gallantry of the President and his children.

So it was not unusual for the Gardiners to attend a small gathering of 13 people at the White House on the evening of February 7, 1843. The evening's entertainment consisted of playing whist, a card game, but it was so cold in the Red

Room of the White House that the guests could barely hold their cards.

The President arrived about 9:30 P.M. in a particularly jovial mood, and he began to tease Julia about the number of boyfriends she had. Then he asked her to join him in a two-handed card game. After the other guests had departed, the President invited the Gardiners to linger for a few hours in front of a fire in the family quarters. By the time the evening was over, John Tyler had made up his mind to get to know the 22-year-old Julia much better.

The President Proposes

Though surrounded by his family, Tyler had been very lonely after Letitia's death. Julia's sparkle and excitement seemed to give the 55-year-old President a new vigor. Like a man 30 years younger, he began to pursue Julia, and before the end of February, he proposed to her. At first, Julia refused. She even hesitated telling her father about the proposal. As she explained, "I feared that he would blame me for allowing the President to have reached the proposing point, so I did not speak of it to anyone."

The President made no attempt to keep his feelings private, and rumors of the romance soon swept Washington. It did not take long for Tyler's ardent pursuit of the fair Julia to win her over. By mid-March, she had agreed to the marriage and her parents were informed.

Though pleased about the marriage, Juliana was not in any hurry to see her daughter married quickly. The President had hoped for a November wedding, but the wise Juliana insisted on her daughter's waiting to make sure that Julia's feelings were genuine and that she had not been swept off her feet by the President's charm and the idea of becoming First Lady.

Taking an Interest in Politics

While the Gardiner family returned to East Hampton, New York, for the summer months, the Tyler clan visited Sherwood Forest, their new home on the James River. All summer the letters flowed back and forth, between Tyler and Julia, with Tyler writing loving descriptions of the home to which he hoped to bring his future bride.

On Julia's previous visits to Washington, she had attended sessions of the Senate and the House of Representatives, but she had found the experiences rather dull. On describing one visit, she remarked, "I was about as wise when I finished as to who voted upon either side as when he commenced." This time, when the Gardiner family returned to Washington for the 1843–1844 winter, Julia took a much more serious interest in the administration's political problems and activities.

As Tyler's administration moved into its final year, most of the furor over the tariff and land distribution issues died down. The President was feeling more relaxed than he had been for some time, and the prospect of his coming marriage to Julia gave rise to feelings of more happiness in the future.

TRAGEDY STRIKES

The dream of a calm ending to Tyler's administration and a new life with Julia was shattered on February 22, 1844. The new pride of the United States Navy was a steam-powered frigate called the *Princeton*. Its captain, Robert Stockton, had invited over 400 people for a gala party aboard the ship. Among the honored guests were Senator Gardiner and his daughters, Cabinet members, U.S. senators and congressmen, and foreign diplomats. A sumptuous feast had been prepared and the highlight of the affair was to be the firing of the world's largest naval gun, the "Peacemaker."

The explosion of the "Peacemaker" aboard the naval frigate
Princeton *on February 28, 1844. Both Secretary of State Abel*
Upshur and Senator David Gardiner were killed in the acci-
dent. President Tyler and his bride-to-be, Julia Gardiner, es-
caped injury because they were below, dining with other
members of the party. (Library of Congress.)

It was about 3:00 P.M. when the guests were invited to
the ship's salon for food and drink. Julia had lingered on the
deck until the President sent an aide to fetch her. The President then began a series of champagne toasts to the new ship,
to its captain, and to the new gun.

After Tyler's toasts, Secretary of the Navy Thomas Gilmer suggested that the big gun now be fired (it had already
been tested twice before). Captain Stockton agreed and went
on deck, followed by a group of gentlemen. The President
was detained below for a few moments, sparing his life. For
as the gun was fired, it exploded, spraying jagged chunks of
red-hot iron around the deck.

As the black smoke billowed into the salon, a cry was heard, "The secretary of state is dead!" In a panic, Julia tried to rush to her father's side to see if he was all right. When she heard, "You can do no good. Your father is in heaven," she fainted. Tyler carried the unconscious Julia to a rescue boat that was alongside the *Princeton*.

The President was devastated by the loss of Secretary of State Upshur as well as Secretary Gilmer and Julia's father. The bodies of those who died in the tragic accident lay in state in the East Room of the White House; funeral services were held on Capitol Hill.

A Secret Wedding

After Julia left Washington on March 5, the President was overwhelmed with loneliness. Julia, too, must have been very lonely, for seven weeks after her father was buried, she informed the President that she was ready to marry him. The secret wedding took place on June 26, 1844.

Two months earlier, in April, a group of Tyler's friends had met in a convention in Baltimore and nominated him for another term. The platform on which Tyler would run was "Tyler and Texas." The issue of the annexation of Texas would be the last great battle of his presidency. With him would be a strong and adoring ally, Julia Gardiner Tyler.

Chapter 10

Texas but Not Tyler

For five years, Texans had waited, hoping to be invited to Washington. Texas had won its independence from Mexico in April 1836 and had declared itself the Republic of Texas following the battle of San Jacinto. The people of Texas, mostly men and women who had emigrated from the United States, were eager to have the new republic unite with their former homeland. When asked to vote on a new constitution in September of that year, an overwhelming number of Texans championed annexation with the United States.

By early 1837, the United States, England, France, and several other European powers had all recognized the new republic. During that same year, Texas, under the leadership of its president, Sam Houston, made two offers to join the United States. Both were turned down. Angered by these rejections, Houston withdrew the offer and no other action was taken until after Tyler became President.

Two more times, in 1842, the new republic offered annexation and was rebuffed. The issue of slavery was being hotly debated in Congress, and the North refused to consider the idea that another slave-holding state might be added to the union.

FLIRTING WITH ENGLAND

Now Sam Houston began a series of new tactics. Instead of playing the role of suitor, Texas would play the role of flirt. The object of this flirtation was Great Britain. Economic conditions in Texas were getting worse. Mexico sat on the sidelines, waiting for the new republic to falter and hoping that it might regain the territory it had lost. Texas needed the support of a strong ally. Great Britain, already in control of Canada, seemed more than willing to ally itself with another piece of real estate on the North American continent.

Tyler had long been a supporter of Texas annexation, but his secretary of state, Daniel Webster, was not. In 1842, when Texas had made its two offers to the United States, the Webster–Ashburton Treaty was being negotiated. Tyler conceded that annexing Texas at this time might jeopardize the agreement with England. When Webster resigned in 1843, President Tyler appointed his good friend, Abel P. Upshur, as secretary of state. Upshur matched Tyler in his enthusiasm for annexing Texas, and conditions in the United States seemed to favor a change of heart regarding Texas.

Flirtation Pays Off

Houston's flirtation began to pay off. Both Tyler and Upshur were convinced that having England allied with Texas would threaten the security of the American Southwest. Many of the southern states were beginning to worry that Great Britain's antislavery policy might compel Texas to abolish the institution. Southerners feared that slaves from the South might escape to Texas and there would be conflicts with Texans as southerners tried to reclaim their property.

This time, it was Upshur who offered annexation, and Houston who rejected it. He let it be known that some Euro-

Sam Houston was the first president of the Republic of Texas.
On several occasions, Texas offered to annex itself to the
United States but Congress turned down the offer each time.
However, Tyler's persistent efforts to bring Texas into the
Union finally resulted in a joint agreement on March 1, 1845,
just three days before the end of Tyler's term of office. (Library
of Congress.)

pean governments were arranging a peace treaty between Texas and Mexico, guaranteeing the independence of Texas. Houston explained that he could not be expected "to abandon the expectations which now exist of a speedy settlement of our difficulties with Mexico . . . for the very uncertain prospects of annexation to the United States."

Upshur Ups His Offer

During the Webster-Ashburton negotiations, Webster had met with senators behind the scenes, trying to find out how they planned to vote on the treaty. Such a practice is common today, but not in Tyler's time. Webster had been so successful in learning the strength of his votes in the Senate that Upshur decided to try the same tactic to determine the Senate's interest in annexing Texas. His quiet polling of the senators convinced him that the Senate favored annexation, and he reported to Tyler that there would be enough votes for the two-thirds majority needed to pass the annexation treaty.

Upshur directed W.S. Murphy, the U.S. representative in Texas, to inform Houston that the annexation measure would pass the Senate and that the United States would send naval forces to the Gulf of Mexico and station American troops on the southwestern border should Mexico send forces against Texas during negotiations. However, before Houston's negotiator could reach Washington, Upshur died in the *Princeton* explosion.

TWO REGRETTABLE EVENTS

The last person Tyler would have chosen for his secretary of state was John C. Calhoun. Of all the Cabinet appointments made by Tyler, this was the one he most regretted. But his hand was forced by the meddling of one of his dearest friends, Henry A. Wise.

After the tragedy of the *Princeton*, the attorney general, John Nelson, acted temporarily as secretary of state, giving Tyler an opportunity to make his permanent choice. In the meantime, Wise felt that Calhoun would make an excellent candidate. Moreover, Wise was indebted to a South Carolina friend of Calhoun's, Senator George McDuffie. Without discussing the matter with Tyler, Wise took it upon himself to see McDuffie and suggested Calhoun for the open Cabinet position. McDuffie, assuming that the offer had come from the President, proceeded to write to Calhoun.

When Wise informed Tyler of the steps he had taken, the President was rightfully infuriated. Tyler knew that Calhoun could bring few supporters to Texas annexation, and that his appointment would signal "slavery" to many of the northern senators. If the Texas annexation was successful, Tyler also fretted that the ambitious Calhoun might end up getting credit for what was Tyler's achievement. But the President could not bring himself to break with Wise, his old personal friend and strongest political ally.

On March 6, 1844, Tyler's appointment of John Calhoun as his new secretary of state was unanimously passed by the Senate. All the groundwork that Upshur had laid now paid off—for Calhoun. The treaty of annexation was signed on April 12. According to its provisions, the citizens of Texas would enjoy "all the rights, privileges, and immunities, of citizens of the United States." All the lands of Texas would become part of the United States and, in return, the United States would take over the $10 million debt of Texas.

Tyler Says too Much

Ten days later, the annexation document was submitted to the Senate for approval. Along with it was a message from the President and a series of papers in support of the treaty. Tyler argued that with its good soil and climate, Texas would soon be a wealthy addition to the country. Commerce and coastal trade would benefit both the South and the North. Further, he noted that if the United States did not accecpt Texas, the new republic would look to other nations for security and for trade.

Had Tyler stopped there, the battle might have been won. Unfortunately, he went on to argue the southern cause. He stated that Great Britain might try to push Texas into agreeing to abolish slavery in order to be guaranteed peace with Texas. Instead of limiting his arguments to those that affected the entire nation, Tyler's pro-South statements created sectional conflicts and antagonized the North.

By this time, the 1844 presidential election was in full swing. Henry Clay, the Whig candidate, came out strongly against annexation. The Democratic candidate, James Polk, favored annexation, but Democrats were in the minority. When every Whig but one voted against the treaty, the measure failed to pass the Senate.

Tyler refused to accept defeat. Polk's victory in the presidential election and the increase in Democratic ranks proved to Tyler that the American public favored annexation. Individuals and state legislatures were petitioning for union with Texas. The issue could not be ignored by Congress.

In his annual State of the Union message delivered in December 1844, Tyler made a new recommendation. It was doubtful that the present Senate, dominated by Whigs, would approve the treaty, which required two-thirds vote. Since he had Democratic support in the House of Representatives, the President suggested that annexation be accepted by a joint resolution of both Houses, requiring only a simple majority.

VICTORY BUT NOT VINDICATION

The suggestion was picked up. The approved joint resolution arrived on the President's desk on March 1, 1845, just three days before he would turn over the reins of government to James Knox Polk, the 11th President of the United States. The treaty passed by both houses was more favorable to Texas than the one written by Calhoun. Texas would pay her own debt, but in an unusual arrangement that is unique among the current 50 states, Texas would retain title to its public lands.

At the last moment, the document had been amended solely to appease one or two senators. Time was running out for both the annexation treaty and for Tyler. If the treaty were resubmitted for further negotiations, it might never be signed, certainly not in time for Tyler's administration to receive the credit. At a meeting with the Cabinet on March 2, it was agreed that there could be no delay. As a courtesy to the incoming President, Calhoun was sent to inform Polk of the decision and to seek out his opinion. Polk listened but refused to give any opinion or make any suggestions.

Saving the Treaty

Instructions were sent to Andrew Jackson Donelson, the new U.S. representative in Texas. One of the reasons that Donelson had been chosen for the position was that he was a nephew of Andrew Jackson's wife. Tyler had sought Jackson's support during the negotiations on Texas, and the old hero of New Orleans and former President had done his part in encouraging annexation. Donelson had turned out to be a most effective representative.

Donelson had warned that there was an urgent need to complete the treaty as soon as possible because the British and the French were also working on a treaty between Texas and Mexico. One provision of that treaty was that Texas would promise never to unite with any other nation. Should the British–French treaty be signed, the idea of unification with the United States would be dead for all time.

Tyler's prompt action saved the treaty. Texas was now forced to decide whether it wanted independence and peace with Mexico or union with the United States. On July 4, 1845, Texans called a special convention at which they declared for annexation. It lacked but one vote to make it unanimous.

The Credit and the Glory

Just as Tyler had feared, much of the credit for the annexation of Texas was given to Calhoun. In a speech in the Senate in 1847, Senator Thomas Benton lauded his old friend Calhoun for his role as the main instigator of annexation. Calhoun did not hesitate to take credit for the event, untruthfully adding that it was *his* idea to use the House resolution for passage of the treaty. When Sam Houston credited Jackson for the success of annexation, Tyler replied that *he* had begun negotiations before seeking Jackson's support.

Not only did Tyler fail to receive credit for his achievement, he also was targeted for criticism by the anti-Texas forces. This group accused the President of annexing Texas for the purpose of opening more land to slavery. They also charged that Tyler's action would lead to war with Mexico.

There were some, however, who appreciated Tyler's efforts. On July 8, 1845, the convention in Texas adopted resolutions thanking Tyler and his Cabinet for their efforts on behalf of the annexation of Texas, and both a county and a county seat in Texas were named after him. He even received a silver pitcher as a New Year's gift from the ladies of Brazoria, Texas, for his role in the annexation.

Chapter 11

A Reputation Regained

The last seven months of President Tyler's administration were crowned by the success of the Texas annexation and a social life in the White House that had not been seen since the days of Dolley Madison. Like a queen, Julia Tyler, the new First Lady, presided over a social season that delighted both local society and official Washington.

Until Julia's arrival, Tyler's natural social inclinations had been hampered by a shortage of funds. An uncooperative Congress refused to give him the usual amounts for new furnishings in the White House. And on state occasions, the President had been forced to pay for fuel and lights from his own funds. But Julia, backed by the Gardiner money, was perfectly willing to pay the necessary expenses for the presidential mansion.

Where previously Tyler had been forced to dress his coachmen in used uniforms, Julia now purchased elegant new uniforms trimmed in black velvet. She ordered expensive French wines and expensive French furniture, and she introduced the polka, a new dance that was the rage of New York. For a man who had found the waltz immoral only a few years earlier, John Tyler, under the influence of his new bride, began to mellow.

But Julia was more than a mere decoration at the White House. While Tyler fought for Texas annexation in his own way, Julia used her charm and powers of persuasion at dinner parties and other social events to gain support for her husband's interests. She was a natural-born lobbyist for her husband's causes.

A PRESIDENT WITH A PARTY

On New Year's Day, 1845, more than 2,000 people presented themselves to the President and the First Lady at a large public reception. The only noticeable absentees among the Washington elite were members of the Whig Party, who were attending a competing affair at the home of John Quincy Adams. One journalist reported after the presidential reception that "President Tyler will go out of the White House with drums beating and colors flying."

Two months later, at the end of February, Julia gave a glorious farewell ball, to which everyone in Washington society sought an invitation. More than 1,000 candles illuminated the four large public rooms used for dancing and promenading. A superb buffet was served and champagne flowed. Presiding over the proceedings was the First Lady, in a white satin and silver gown and bedecked in a full set of diamonds. When someone congratulated Tyler on the success of the affair, he laughed and replied, "Yes, they cannot say now that I am *a President without a party.*"

The passage of the annexation of Texas two weeks later added the final crowning achievement to Tyler's last days in office.

HOME TO SHERWOOD FOREST

On March 4, 1845, President John Tyler rode in the same carriage accompanying the newly elected President, James Polk, to his inauguration. A day later, the Tylers departed for their home in Virginia.

For someone who had enjoyed the glamour and excitement of Washington society as much as Julia had, it might seem that life on a southern plantation might become a bit stifling. But that was never the case with Julia. She threw herself into the planning and management of Sherwood Forest with the same enthusiasm that she had shown in the White House.

The plantation to which Tyler brought his new wife consisted of 1,150 acres and was located on the James River, about 35 miles from Richmond. The house was decorated to Julia's taste, and she soon found her new setting to be a rural paradise.

Road Overseer

Initially, the former President was not to find the same serenity. His neighbors let their political displeasure be known by appointing him to the lowly position of overseer of the road on which he lived. If they intended to humiliate Tyler, they were disappointed, for Tyler turned the tables on them in his own gracious style.

As overseer of the road, he could summon neighbors who lived on the road to do repair work whenever he deemed it necessary. He did this so often that the neighbors soon asked him to resign. But with tongue in cheek, Tyler replied that "offices were hard to obtain in these times and having no assurance that he would ever get another, he could not think, under the circumstances of resigning."

Despite their political differences, it did not take long for the attitude of his neighbors to change. Tyler's courtesy and good nature, and lack of malice to his former enemies, soon won them over.

In Exile

Though he had achieved cordial relations with his neighbors, Tyler had yet to be considered anything but a political failure by his former Washington associates. While other former Presidents might be sought out for advice by former associates or aspiring politicians, few of Tyler's Washington colleagues visited him at Sherwood Forest.

Only once in the next 15 years was he called to the nation's capital, and that was to testify on behalf of Daniel Webster in May 1846. Webster had been accused of mismanagement of funds while he was secretary of state in Tyler's Cabinet. Tyler's testimony, supported by written data in his personal files, impressed the Senate investigating committee and helped to clear Webster's name.

During his stay in Washington while testifying, Tyler was delighted with the positive attention he received. He was invited to Webster's home and had dinner with President Polk at the White House. As a result of this Washington visit, he was later asked to make public addresses at the University of Virginia and at other locations in his home state.

Keeping in Touch

Tyler continued to keep in touch with what was going on in the country. At the time of the Polk election, he had returned to the Democratic Party, and for the rest of his life, he continued to be a loyal party supporter.

At the beginning of Polk's administration, Mexico broke relations with the United States over the annexation of Texas. Polk moved troops to the Texas border, and when open conflict evolved, Tyler strongly backed Polk's decision to declare war against Mexico.

The former President never gave up his dream of returning to public office, possibly as governor, or even as President, but nothing was to come of the half-hearted attempts made on his behalf. However, as time passed, he was received more kindly by his party and the public, and he was offered more opportunities to speak publicly.

Often Julia accompanied her husband on these occasions, even if it meant arriving with two babies and two nurses. Tyler and Julia were to have seven children in the years after 1846, delighting Tyler and keeping Julia very busy.

In 1860 he was asked to deliver a speech at the unveiling of a monument to Henry Clay. Tyler spoke briefly about the differences he had had with Clay, revealing that he had not forgotten the many arrows he had endured from the Kentuckian. But Tyler also revealed his forgiving nature by discussing the positive services Clay had performed for the country, particularly his efforts on behalf of the Compromise Tariff of 1833.

TYLER AS PEACEMAKER

The issue of slavery and northern versus southern interests continued to plague the country. Tyler may have been on the sidelines, but he was a vitally interested observer of what was happening to the country. By means of personal letters to friends and anonymous letters to newspapers, he made his opinions known.

In 1846 Tyler had objected to the Wilmot Proviso, which called for the exclusion of slavery in any new territory acquired from Mexico in the Mexican–American War. In 1850 he was asked by a member of Congress to give his opinion on a compromise—the Compromise of 1850—proposed by his old enemy, Henry Clay. Thinking more of the country's welfare than his personal pride, Tyler endorsed the package, which offered a series of accommodations to satisfy both the North and the South. When the issue was brought before Congress, both Henry Clay, a lean, frail man in his mid-seventies, and Daniel Webster, a robust, theatrical member of the opposition party, spoke to a jam-packed audience in favor of the measure. In the audience was John Calhoun, who feebly tried to interrupt with his objections. Despite Calhoun's attempts and those of other die-hard southerners, Clay's compromise did pass, putting off the inevitable conflict, the Civil War, for more than 10 years.

A Look into the Future

During the 1850s, Tyler's mind may have been occupied with concerns about the Union, but his heart and hands were occupied with his plantation, Julia, and their growing brood of seven active children. By 1860, however, Tyler was deeply worried about the future of the country. States' rights no longer seemed important; what did engage his mind was how the Union could be maintained. On July 4, 1860, he confided to a friend, Thomas Dunn English, that he was "convinced that the South would go to war . . . and that in the end the money, resources, and numerical strength of the North would win." Tyler's prophecy would come true, though death would spare him the agony of witnessing the tragedy.

THE ELECTION OF 1860

The presidential election of 1860 presented a fragmented Democratic Party split by the separate interests of the northern and southern factions. When John Brown, a radical abolitionist (one trying to stop slavery), tried to provoke a slave uprising at the federal arsenal at Harpers Ferry, Virginia, in October 1858, southerners were mobilized by fear. By the time of the Democratic nominating convention, southerners were in no mood for compromise.

The convention was held in Charleston, South Carolina. The favored candidate of northern Democrats was Stephen A. Douglas, a senator from Illinois. But as the convention progressed, one after another of the southern delegations walked out, angered that the party would not endorse the pro-slavery platform they had proposed. When a second Democratic convention was held later in Baltimore, Maryland, many of the southern delegates walked out again. They then reassembled in another hall and proceeded to nominate their own candidate, John C. Breckinridge, who was then Vice-President under President James Buchanan.

By 1860 the power of the Whigs had been replaced by a new party, the Republican Party. And a coalition of southern and northern conservatives, calling themselves the Constitutional Union Party, nominated John Bell of Tennessee.

Tyler was visibly upset by the development of the new Constitutional Union Party and the split in the Democratic Party, fearing that it would lead to the election of Abraham Lincoln, the Republican candidate. He also feared that if Lincoln gained the presidency, South Carolina and the other cotton states would secede from the Union. Tyler's fears were well founded. Shortly after Lincoln won the election, South Carolina, followed by several other states, seceded from the Union.

The Price of Peace

John Tyler was one of several political leaders anxious to prevent a civil war. In January 1861, with Tyler's encouragement, the Virginia legislature called for a peace convention to be held in Washington. Among the Virginia delegates to the convention were John Tyler and William C. Rives. Tyler was commissioned by the Virginia legislature to speak to the President of the United States. At the same time, the legislature commissioned Judge John Robertson to speak to the authorities in the seceded states. Both men were to urge all parties to abstain from "all acts calculated to produce a collision of arms between the States and the Government of the United States" until the peace convention could meet. At a meeting with Buchanan (Lincoln was not inaugurated until March 4, 1861), the President agreed to recommend to Congress that no hostile action be taken until the mediation efforts of Virginia were completed.

The peace conference began on February 4, 1861. Tyler arrived in Washington with Julia and their two youngest children. At 40 years of age, Julia had the same energy she had always displayed. Her return to the nation's capital gave her a delightful opportunity to prove to Washington society that she had not lost any of her beauty, charm, or spirit. Tyler, now 71 years old and in failing health, had a difficult time trying to keep up with his enthusiastic wife.

A Hopeless Situation

On February 5, Tyler was unanimously elected president of the convention. The gathering was to consider a series of proposals which would, upon agreement of the delegates, be offered to Congress. Unfortunately, the convention was doomed to failure. Though the 132 delegates included men who had been Cabinet officers, governors, and congressmen, the free states outnumbered the slave states, and many of the delegates were as old and feeble as Tyler himself.

During February, convention members met with Buchanan. The same courtesy was also extended to President-elect Lincoln. While the meeting with Buchanan was maintained on a social level, the meeting with Lincoln soon turned into a political squabble. Lincoln attempted some humorous comments to lighten the situation, but all it did was to irritate many of the southerners. Several of them attempted to bait Lincoln, even accusing him of supporting such extreme abolitionist actions as the Harpers Ferry raid by John Brown. The situation deteriorated and a number of southerners stormed out. Tyler remained, but when he heard Lincoln say in response to a question about slavery, "In a choice of evils, war may not always be the worst," Tyler viewed the situation as hopeless.

The committee meetings of the peace convention were filled with dissent and angry words, and the watered-down proposals that finally reached the convention floor were voted on half-heartedly, each vote being very close. The group was unable to agree enthusiastically on any proposal. Tyler reluctantly accepted the task of conveying the proposals to Congress, but he had already lost hope. The proposals were rejected by the Senate and failed to get a hearing in the House.

A RETURN TO THE FOLD

Tyler had gone to the peace convention as a pacifist; he returned as an avowed secessionist. On February 18, while the peace convention was still in session, the Confederate States of America had been proclaimed in Montgomery, Alabama, and Jefferson Davis had been inaugurated as president. Even before the peace convention had ended, a state convention assembled in Richmond to consider the secession of Virginia. In his absence, Tyler was elected to the state convention and had taken his seat at the gathering by March 1.

War Begins; Virginia Secedes

Despite the fact that he was exhausted and frail, Tyler urged secession in impassioned speeches that, at times, could hardly be heard. It looked as if some members of the Constitutional Union Party might defeat the secession proposal. Then on April 12, Fort Sumter, a small federal fort in the Charleston, South Carolina, harbor, was fired upon by a Confederate shore battery. The die was cast. On April 17, Lincoln called for

75,000 volunteers for the Union Army and asked Virginia to send her quota.

Virginia's response was to promptly pass an ordinance of secession. On May 23, after secession had been ratified by a vote of the people, the Virginia convention ratified the constitution of the Confederacy, making the state a part of the southern republic. Tyler was chairman of the committee that negotiated Virginia's alliance with the Confederacy.

Tyler had regained the admiration and respect of his fellow Virginians and the South. He was unanimously chosen by the people of Virginia for a seat in the Provisional Congress of the Confederacy. With encouragement and active support from his friends, Tyler, announced that he would be a candidate for the House of Representatives when the new Confederacy went into effect in February 1862. Though there were three other candidates for the position, Tyler won the race easily. But fate prevented his ever taking his seat of office.

A FINAL PEACE

In January 1862, Tyler was in Richmond, busy attending the sessions of the Provisional Congress of the Confederacy. Julia Tyler had planned to join her husband later in the month. But an unexpected dream caused her to arrive a week earlier than planned. In the dream, she saw her husband lying seriously ill, needing her. But when she arrived at the Exchange Hotel with baby Pearl on January 10, she found her husband quite well.

Two days later, however, Tyler awoke feeling nauseous and dizzy. He said he would feel better after having a cup of tea in the hotel dining room. But as he finished the drink and prepared to leave, he fell unconscious. Although he recovered in a few minutes, he remained in his room for the next several days. He had headaches and a cough, but he managed to see visitors and discuss the affairs of the new Confederacy.

Early in the morning hours of January 18, Julia awoke to hear her husband gasping for breath. She quickly summoned a doctor who was staying in the hotel. Baby Pearl, who had been sleeping on a cot next to Julia, began to cry, and Tyler murmured, "Poor little thing, how I disturb her."

As Julia tried to get him to take a sip of brandy, Tyler looked up at her, smiled, and quietly died. Julia later recalled that the bed in which he died "was exactly like the one I saw him in in my dream, and unlike any of our own."

Though Tyler had hoped to be buried in a simple ceremony at Sherwood Forest, he lay in state in the black-draped hall of the Confederate Congress in Richmond. On the day of the funeral, Jefferson Davis, president of the Confederacy, and other southern dignitaries jammed the church, and a train of 150 carriages accompanied the hearse to Hollywood Cemetery. There Tyler was buried next to the tomb of President James Monroe. In Washington, little notice was paid to Tyler's passing, for to the North, he was now "a rebel and a traitor."

Tyler's death may have been an act of charity. He was spared seeing the South overrun by Union forces and his beloved Sherwood Forest home vandalized, its furniture and pictures destroyed. Nor did he have to witness Julia, struggling with a plantation of 1,600 acres and 70 slaves, running a blockade with five bales of cotton and sending four of the older children up North to their grandmother.

In the end, Tyler may have been viewed by the South as a patriot and by the North as a traitor. But he would be remembered best by his family as a man who rode around the plantation in an old floppy straw hat, who bounced babies on his knees, who wrote loving letters to his children, and who wrote poetry to his wife.

Bibliography

Bailey, Thomas A. *The Pugnacious Presidents: White House Warriors on Parade.* New York: The Free Press, 1980. Chapter 10, "John Tyler: The First Accidental President," is an excellent review of Tyler's handling of foreign policy during his presidential years. It also gives good coverage of the Dorr Rebellion in Rhode Island and the Webster-Ashburton Treaty.

Burns, James M. *The Vineyard of Liberty.* New York: Knopf, 1982. Chapters 7–13 give excellent background information on the American scene during the years of Tyler's career from congressman to President. The book presents ideas on slavery, politics, and the economy, in a well-written, readable style.

Chitwood, Oliver P. *John Tyler, Champion of the Old South.* New York: Russell and Russell, 1964. This is the most cited and complete text on the life of Tyler.

Chitwood, Oliver P., Patrick, Rembert W., and Owsley, Frank L. *The American People: A History.* Vol. 1 to 1877. Princeton, NJ: D. Van Nostrand, 1962. Chapter 29, "A President Without a Party," gives a brief overview of Tyler's career, particularly his term as President.

Hicks, John D. *A Short History of American Democracy.* Cambridge, MA: The Riverside Press, 1949. Chapter 13, "The Panic of 1837," describes the economic and political problems created by this depression and John Tyler's role during these years.

Roseboom, Eugene H. *A History of Presidential Elections: From George Washington to Richard M. Nixon.* New York: Macmillan, 1970. A well-written book that gives the background on the issues and the men involved in every presidential election from Washington to Nixon. Chapter 8, "Whigs and Democrats, 1833–1843," contains a good description of the Whig era and its origins.

Seager II, Robert. *And Tyler, Too: A Biography of John and Julia Tyler.* New York: McGraw Hill, 1963. A fascinating story of two families, the Tylers and that of Tyler's second wife, Julia Gardiner. Their marriage joined two prominent families, one from the South and one from the North. There are excellent chapters on the Tyler family and Tyler's career.

Index

PRESIDENTS OF THE UNITED STATES

GEORGE WASHINGTON	L. Falkof	0-944483-19-4
JOHN ADAMS	R. Stefoff	0-944483-10-0
THOMAS JEFFERSON	R. Stefoff	0-944483-07-0
JAMES MADISON	B. Polikoff	0-944483-22-4
JAMES MONROE	R. Stefoff	0-944483-11-9
JOHN QUINCY ADAMS	M. Greenblatt	0-944483-21-6
ANDREW JACKSON	R. Stefoff	0-944483-08-9
MARTIN VAN BUREN	R. Ellis	0-944483-12-7
WILLIAM HENRY HARRISON	R. Stefoff	0-944483-54-2
JOHN TYLER	L. Falkof	0-944483-60-7
JAMES K. POLK	M. Greenblatt	0-944483-04-6
ZACHARY TAYLOR	D. Collins	0-944483-17-8
MILLARD FILLMORE	K. Law	0-944483-61-5
FRANKLIN PIERCE	F. Brown	0-944483-25-9
JAMES BUCHANAN	D. Collins	0-944483-62-3
ABRAHAM LINCOLN	R. Stefoff	0-944483-14-3
ANDREW JOHNSON	R. Stevens	0-944483-16-X
ULYSSES S. GRANT	L. Falkof	0-944483-02-X
RUTHERFORD B. HAYES	N. Robbins	0-944483-23-2
JAMES A. GARFIELD	F. Brown	0-944483-63-1
CHESTER A. ARTHUR	R. Stevens	0-944483-05-4
GROVER CLEVELAND	D. Collins	0-944483-01-1
BENJAMIN HARRISON	R. Stevens	0-944483-15-1
WILLIAM McKINLEY	D. Collins	0-944483-55-0
THEODORE ROOSEVELT	R. Stefoff	0-944483-09-7
WILLIAM H. TAFT	L. Falkof	0-944483-56-9
WOODROW WILSON	D. Collins	0-944483-18-6
WARREN G. HARDING	A. Canadeo	0-944483-64-X
CALVIN COOLIDGE	R. Stevens	0-944483-57-7

HERBERT C. HOOVER	B. Polikoff	0-944483-58-5
FRANKLIN D. ROOSEVELT	M. Greenblatt	0-944483-06-2
HARRY S. TRUMAN	D. Collins	0-944483-00-3
DWIGHT D. EISENHOWER	R. Ellis	0-944483-13-5
JOHN F. KENNEDY	L. Falkof	0-944483-03-8
LYNDON B. JOHNSON	L. Falkof	0-944483-20-8
RICHARD M. NIXON	R. Stefoff	0-944483-59-3
GERALD R. FORD	D. Collins	0-944483-65-8
JAMES E. CARTER	D. Richman	0-944483-24-0
RONALD W. REAGAN	N. Robbins	0-944483-66-6
GEORGE H.W. BUSH	R. Stefoff	0-944483-67-4

GARRETT EDUCATIONAL CORPORATION
130 EAST 13TH STREET
ADA, OK 74820